SALMON RUN

SALMON RUN

JACK CHARLTON

with Tony Francis

STANLEY PAUL

London

Stanley Paul & Co. Ltd

An imprint of the Random Century Group
20 Vauxhall Bridge Road, London SW1V 2SA

Random Century Australia (Pty) Ltd
20 Alfred Street, Milsons Point, Sydney 2061

Random Century New Zealand Limited
191 Archers Road, PO Box 40-086, Auckland 10

Random Century South Africa (Pty) Ltd
PO Box 337, Bergvlei 2012, South Africa

First published 1992

Set in Frutiger by 🅐 Tek Art Ltd,
Addiscombe, Croydon, Surrey

Printed and bound by Clays Ltd, St. Ives PLC

A catalogue record for this book is available upon
request from the British Library

ISBN 0 09 177264 8

PHOTOGRAPH ACKNOWLEDGEMENTS

The majority of photographs in this book are by
courtesy of Yorkshire Television (Kenneth Martin and
Stephen Daniels), Tony Francis and Kingfisher
Productions. Thanks are also due to the following for
allowing the use of copyright photographs:

Roger Archibald/Oxford Scientific Films, J.T.
Brownlee/Teviot Smokery, Fred Buller, Terry Cobb,
Rob Cousins/Susan Griggs Agency, Jeff Foott/Oxford
Scientific Films, Peter Gray/Kielder Hatchery, Glenn
Harvey/Camera Press, Hereford City Museum,
Johnny Johnson/Oxford Scientific Films, Alain Le
Garsmeur/Landscape Only, Arthur Oglesby, Syndica-
tion International, Topham Picture Library, Adam
Woolfitt/Susan Griggs Agency, Charlie Wright

CONTENTS

THE KING OF FISH

Welcome to our expedition. We're off in search of the most amazing creature on earth and the legions of people who fall under its spell. The salmon, otherwise known as the king of fish, remains one of life's great mysteries. In between hatching and perishing in our rivers, it ventures thousands of miles out to sea for food. Why? How does it find its way back to the river of origin? Why does it go for a fly when it's not interested in food once it's back in fresh-water?

MY IDEA OF HEAVEN. WADING IN A SALMON POOL AND ANTICIPATING THE THRILL OF THE TAKE. TIME JUST STANDS STILL

The salmon defies logic. It offers the sportsman the most exciting challenge of all. Why else would we spend thousands of pounds each year trying to catch it? The economy of some parts of Scotland depends on it. For all that, we come back empty-handed as often as not. I suppose that's the magic. If salmon was as easy to catch as trout we wouldn't be so bewitched. I heard of one guy who went four years without a catch during his annual week on the river Dee but was still as keen as mustard each time he returned.

This book, as you'll discover, isn't about catching fish. You might pick up a few tips

SALMON FISHING'S BECOME ÉLITIST BUT THERE ARE STILL PLACES WHERE YOU CAN GO WITHOUT RE-MORTGAGING YOUR HOUSE

along the way but that isn't really the point of the exercise. When Tony Francis asked me at the end of Ireland's World Cup campaign what subject I'd choose for another television series, I had no hesitation. 'The world's great salmon pools,' I told him. And that's how it all started. I wanted to visit Glendelvine Water on the Tay and see for myself where Georgina Ballantine caught the biggest salmon ever taken in British waters. I wanted to meet the Royal family's head ghillie at Balmoral and listen to his tales. I also wanted to find out where all the salmon had gone from that most pictures-que of rivers, the Wye, running between England and Wales; and how the drift net

fishermen of Northumberland justified a business that was banned in most other parts of the world.

We ran into poachers in Northumberland and in Wales, and were lucky enough to see salmon spawning in the north Tyne, not far from where I live – one of the most wonderful sights you could imagine. And it was a great pleasure to meet Arthur Oglesby, one of this country's most respected salmon fishermen, on Norway's famous river Orkla. We fished under the midnight sun but didn't take a single salmon!

The highlight undoubtedly was our week in Alaska. What a contrast! Local residents were being urged to catch as many sockeye salmon as they could by whatever means they chose to prevent the lakes and riverbeds from clogging up with rotting carcasses!

Alaska is where we came across Pacific salmon which are even more intriguing than Atlantic salmon. There are five species to start with. We caught three of them – sockeye, chum and king salmon. Fishing on the mighty Kenai river south of Anchorage was unforgettable. The whole town of Soldotna seemed to be there, either wading or in boats in one huge midsummer jamboree. The glacier-fed river was a milky turquoise in colour. The salmon were running in their thousands.

We had a taste of fear too. A one-mile trek through the woods with Alaskan brown bears likely to spring out at any moment was, to say the least, unnerving. But when we eventually made it to the waterfall where the bears were feeding on sockeye, we agreed it had been worth the risk.

All in all, it was an experience I shall always treasure. We met some fascinating characters, from the 70-year-old Alaskan pilot who never bothers with navigational equipment, to the Scottish professor who believes cock salmon are sexually attracted to women; from the fish restaurateur in County Galway who held the world oyster-eating record, to the Welsh poacher who said the only way he could pay his fines was to keep poaching!

Love them or dislike them, they all belong to the world of salmon fishing. A remarkable world full of history and legend, debate and counter-debate. Let the journey begin. . . .

CHAPTER ONE

RICH MAN, POOR MAN

Through the Middle Ages the Scottish rivers teemed with salmon and people took it for granted. Some even got sick of it. One of Cromwell's soldiers sent a letter from the river Forth in the seventeenth century, saying: 'Here the burgomasters are compelled to reinforce an ancient statute that commands all masters not to force any servant or apprentice to feed upon salmon more than thrice a week.'

Until the railways opened up Britain in Victorian times salmon fishing as a commercial sport hardly existed. Landlords were doing so

TWO – NIL! EARLY MORNING AT STOBHALL. BEATS LIKE THIS ARE OUT OF REACH OF THE ORDINARY MAN . . .

well out of farming and forestry that they didn't need to look to fishing and sport as a major source of estate income. All that has changed. Today some estates would be in big trouble without the salmon. Many of them have sold their beats on a timeshare basis and others are desperate to keep up the seasonal kill because high figures attract more paying customers. Some estates are insisting you fish a minimum number of hours so the records look as good as possible. Arthur Oglesby tells me that on one of the estates where he fishes his contract says that he must fish not less than seven hours a day or he might lose his tenancy. 'What a way to run a resource!' says Arthur. Strange, isn't it? Salmon is the most threatened species in our fisheries and yet it's the one we try to kill in ever greater numbers year by year.

Only the wealthy can hope to get on the best beats, or even join the queues to get on, but if you're a public figure or a captain of industry you'll probably jump those too. I know it's true because I have. The prospects for the ordinary man or woman are pretty dim. Apart from the money question the average working person in England has no salmon rivers within easy reach. If he wants to fish he has to go to Scotland where three-quarters of the salmon in British waters are to be found, and even if he could afford the time and the petrol, the chances of getting on a half decent beat have long since vanished.

And what's more, Saturday's his only chance because fishing on the Sabbath's banned.

A pal of mine made his fortune in open-cast mining in the Midlands. When he was a lad he used to drive 500 miles to Tayside on a Friday night after work; sleep in the car to save money; fish all day Saturday and set off home again on Sunday to be ready for work the next day. That's how much he loved his salmon fishing. Now a millionaire, he's paid £300,000 for a week's timeshare in perpetuity on one of the best beats, so that his descendants can continue to enjoy its privileges. Why not if he's such a dedicated fisherman and can pay that sort of price?

Ten miles downstream you find the other extreme at the Perth Town Water. There you can fish to your heart's content for £5 a year – and you might catch something. You certainly won't be lonely. There are dozens of fishermen wading side by side. Almost next door is Almondmouth, where Lord Mansfield of Scone Palace has allowed the Stormont Angling Club to fish since 1980. There were nearly six hundred members when I was there, each paying an annual fee of £70, many of them skilful fishermen, casting with eighteen-

... BUT BEATS LIKE THIS AREN'T. JUST A FEW MILES DOWN-STREAM FROM STOBHALL IS THE PERTH TOWN WATER WHERE YOU CAN FISH THE TAY FOR £70 A YEAR

foot rods. The club was very grateful to Lord Mansfield. It's great to see places like that where people can go at a reasonable cost. I love fishing from the bank on that sort of water, and I'd sooner do it than haul or spin all day in a boat on Stobhall for twenty or thirty times the money. Sadly, the locals have no other choice any more. One of the members, Colin Laing, recalled how locals used to be able to fish upriver after 6 p.m. when the tenants had finished their sport. Now that chance has been denied them because a lot of the Scone estate river's been sold to timeshare. The lads from the Stormont Club are philosophical: 'Farming's declined so the estate has to look to whatever means it can to survive,' said Colin.

Lord Stormont, son of Lord Mansfield, was hoping to raise nearly £3 million for sixteen timeshare weeks on Fishponds and over £4 million for fourteen weeks on Waulkmill. A prime beat for the mid-week of September was on offer for £700,000. Not surprisingly business was a bit slow. We invited father and son to put the case for timeshare and defend allegations that riparian landowners were getting greedy. They refused unless Kingfisher Television Productions, the company making the television series, paid £1,000 into an estate charity called Stormont Bequest.

For £1,500 I fish for a week in September at Stobhall. I know it's a lot of money, but I'm putting a few bob back into the Scottish economy — staying in local hotels, buying cigars and whisky from the local shops. I spend the week with a great fishing buddy of long standing, Ray Bailey, a businessman from Telford and director of Shrewsbury Town Football Club. He's been going to Stobhall for eight years. Since timeshare started on the Tay the river's never been so well looked after and hoteliers and shopkeepers have never had it so good. A recent survey estimates the Scottish economy benefits to the tune of £50 million a year from salmon fishing. Five thousand jobs depend on it.

Ray's got the time and money to enjoy the best but he's got mixed feelings about timeshare. It's the social problems it creates that worry him most:

'Timeshare affords privilege to the few. I don't like that because many families who've fished Scottish rivers for donkeys' years will never be able to again. And it offends me that a lot of people take a timeshare week purely as an investment to sell on at a later date. If people want to buy pictures or fill their cellars with vintage port, that's fine, it hurts no one. It gives the auctioneers and wine merchants a living. To take away for selfish ends local people's right to fish is wrong.'

But wait a minute. Hadn't Ray himself bought a timeshare week?

'No, a debenture. That gives us permission to fish the river for three days every October for the next eight years. I get first choice.'

If rivers are to be protected, though, surely we can't let everyone fish them? To that extent timeshare serves a purpose.

'Yes, but let's make sure not all the days are taken. Let's release some for local people. That'll give fishing a better name. It's getting an awful reputation now because of the "hooray Henrys".'

What about the 'hooray Henrys' who are *selling* timeshares?

'Those people are the most offensive of all.

Four or five years ago, before the Big Crash, people from the City, twenty-six- and twenty-seven-year-olds who knew nothing about fishing and had no interest in it whatever, came along and bought stretches of river as if they were going out of fashion.'

That's an accusation you certainly can't level at the royal family. They've enjoyed one of the most privileged salmon beats in the world ever since Queen Victoria and the Prince Consort fell in love with Balmoral. Actually the royal couple were more interested in mountain walks than fishing. The present Queen Mother became a most enthusiastic salmon angler and

RECOGNIZE HER? IT'S THE QUEEN MOTHER SALMON FISHING AS THE DUCHESS OF YORK IN 1927

NO MISTAKE THIS TIME. THE QUEEN MOTHER WAS STILL SALMON FISHING UNTIL QUITE RECENTLY

had a new fishing hut built at Birkhall for her eightieth birthday. This beautiful river is not noted for big fish but she has a good record on it. Her biggest was *twenty-eight pounds*.

They actually let me loose on Balmoral for a morning. What a romantic setting. No wonder the prince and the kindergarten teacher fell in love. Actually Princess Di didn't really take to the sport. I expect she'd sooner look around the shops in Aberdeen like most fishermen's wives! At the far end of the Balmoral stretch is an odd-shaped cottage alongside the Old Brig o' Dee where I called in to see Charlie Wright who has ghillied for the Queen Mother for the best part of half a century. It was April and the air was certainly sharp up there. The weekend skiers were out at Glenshee. The

melting snow was sending heavy water tumbling down through the valley. Great place! No wonder Charlie couldn't bring himself to retire from ghillying. He tried once in 1983 but was still working March–June in 1991. It was his way of life. I wanted to know if the Queen Mother was any good.

'Excellent. One of the best lady fishers that ever came here. She's not been casting for a few years now but she knew this river every bit as well as I did. I remember one time at a pool called the Suspension Bridge she caught a lively fourteen-pound salmon and played it superbly. That was her toughest one.'

'What about Prince Charles?'

His face lit up at the mention of his namesake:

'I've known him since he was a boy. He's an excellent fly fisherman. He refuses to put a spinner in his hand. No way.'

'And Princess Di. Does she fish?'

'She started. With a bit of practice she'd have been all right.'

'Did she lose interest?'

'No, but she hasn't been here for a year or two. She never caught a fish when she was with me but once caught two salmon on a river further north.'

Sandy Thompson ghillies on the opposite bank from Balmoral and sees a lot of the royal family too. His stone cottage is in a perfect position with views of Lochnagar one way and a distant view of Balmoral Castle the other. Two hundred metres across the field is the river Dee. What a prospect! He told me:

'I watched Princess Di one day getting lessons from Charlie at the Suspension Bridge. She stayed for about two hours but it didn't look as though her heart was in it. Women don't like standing around. They get bored. Di did.'

Quite a character, Sandy. He told me a lovely story about an old colonel he was ghillying for one day. The colonel hooked a fish and to save him wading Sandy volunteered to net it. The Queen Mother came along the opposite bank and sat on a seat to watch. When Sandy brought off a deft piece of netting, Her Majesty called 'Well done' and clapped. Sandy replied, 'Thank you, ma'am' and waded back to the shore. 'Who was that?' the colonel demanded to know. When Sandy told him the old boy sprang to attention and saluted, almost falling into the river in the process.

The wind was getting up so Sandy suggested we broke for lunch at the fishing hut. The chimney was smoking. The retired bankers who'd taken that week on Sandy's beat had got a good fire going. The whisky was flowing too. It was what you might call a typical salmon fishing scene. There'd been no catches for any of them. People are always telling me they don't mind because they come for the scenery, the camaraderie, etc., but what's the point of spending all that money year after year if they're not catching fish?

WITH A BIT OF PRACTICE PRINCESS DI WOULD HAVE BEEN ALL RIGHT. CHARLIE WRIGHT HAD MORE SUCCESS WITH HIS NAMESAKE

BALMORAL'S HEAD GAMEKEEPER AND GHILLIE HAS SPENT A LIFETIME WITH THE ROYAL FAMILY IN THEIR MOST RELAXED MOMENTS

'Depends how old you are,' replied one of the bankers. 'I've caught a number in the past and when you're not catching you can at least compensate by thinking back to the ones you got before.'

Sitting there by the warmth of the fire, sipping malt and waiting to get back to the banks of one of Britain's finest salmon rivers, you couldn't help but feel privileged. But why should this be out of bounds to the ordinary man? A former employee of the Bank of England gave me yet another perspective on the problem:

'It's frightfully difficult to get on a beat like this. You start off as the low man on the totem pole and as someone dies you move up. You could be on the bottom beat for ten years until you start to move. After fifty years you might get a good week!'

Of course, paying big money to fish for salmon doesn't mean you'll catch any fish – no one can promise that. But what you will get is the guarantee of privacy on a beat where the chances of a catch are much greater. Personally speaking I don't need privacy when I fish.

I'm happy in the crowd at Almondmouth, as I was happy at the public places I've fished in in Norway, Alaska and Ireland.

However, the privacy was exactly what Mark Hudson enjoyed about Balmoral. I didn't realize the royal beats were to let. Fancy being able to tell your mates you fish at Balmoral every year! Mark's a businessman from Cheshire and we found him on a lovely, fast-running stretch of river about halfway between the Brig o' Dee and the Castle. I was dying to know how on earth he'd got permission. The answer was quite simple:

'We used to fish further down the river; then one year in the mid-seventies there was a mix-up in the bookings which left us without a week. I rang around all the factors on the Dee but there was nothing doing. We were in a jam because the hotel was already booked. In desperation I phoned the factor at Balmoral. To my amazement he offered us a week and we've been coming ever since.'

Mark pays much less than I'd have imagined, around £2,000 for a week in April. That's cheaper than many beats I can think of. If the Queen's running the estate as a commercial concern to make a profit she needs to be a bit sharper than that. Mark and his wife and son have only once gone away without salmon. They caught fourteen one year, but he says the most enjoyable was 1978:

'The water was low and when it's like that it's the most lovely river for fly fishing. We caught ten salmon all to the fly. A marvellous year, never to be forgotten.'

The water was much higher when I was there. Catching fish wouldn't be easy. Mark let me borrow his rod for half an hour. While we stood there in the pale sunshine with Charlie Wright keeping an eye on us, we started to discuss the cost of fishing, which is steadily rising while the numbers of salmon are dwindling. I remembered Arthur Oglesby telling me how in the 'good old days' he wanted one fish a day, but today's fishermen have to be content with one fish a week. And yet the landlords feel justified in putting the rents up

QUEEN VICTORIA AND THE PRINCE CONSORT FIRST FELL IN LOVE
WITH BALMORAL ALTHOUGH THEY DIDN'T FISH

because the queue of people wanting to fish gets longer. In 1990 Arthur calculated that the fourteen salmon he caught in eight weeks on the Tay cost him £3,600 each, including accommodation but excluding petrol and drinks in the bar. Contrast that with 1966 when Arthur and two pals had a beat on the Lune which cost them £500 for the season. They took 195 salmon between them! I put it to Mark that there must be a cut-off point. People won't pay more and more for less and less ad infinitum. For goodness' sake, every salmon caught by rod and line nowadays is reckoned to cost £5,000!

'Well people have more money to spend and more leisure time. Fishing like this is within the reach of more people than it was twenty to thirty years ago, but whether they'll go on paying five thousand pounds a fish I doubt. But the cost wouldn't stop me coming.'

'Yes but you'd only come in the expectation of catching a fish – not just to enjoy the countryside?'

'I agree.'

The Ardo beat on the Dee used to be the property of Mr McKenzie Smith, who also owned the Ardo House hotel, but he sold it in 1989 when timeshare was peaking, to Jim Slater's company, Salar Properties, which ruled the market. According to Colonel Bob Campbell, the chairman of the Dee District Salmon Fishery, Salar bought the beat for £280,000 and 'timeshared' it for £4½ million.

'I consider it a disgrace,' was Colonel Campbell's view. 'They introduced twelve rods onto a beat which should only have six and they were sold in perpetuity. That's overfishing. Bad practice. Forty thousand pounds per rod in the height of the season. That's nearly half a million a week on a beat worth only a tenth of that. Families are priced out of it – and families who've grown up using a beat are the best people to look after it.'

Strong stuff. And not far from Ardo is Banchory Lodge, a lovely comfortable hotel with its own water. The owner, Dougal Jaffrey, has actually stated in his will that Banchory Lodge water will never be sold to timeshare. He said:

'We're not that type of people. We don't want to abandon it to the highest bidder and lie in the sun on a Caribbean island. We *care* about the river.'

Time for a confession. These days I can fish with lords and ladies but there's still a rascal deep inside me. My uncle Buck used to be a poacher and I've done the odd little bit myself. I remember him asking me one day when I was a nipper:

'Can you swim Jack?'

'No,' I said.

'Well get yourself learned because I'm getting a bit old for going in the water.'

'What do you mean?'

'Someone's got to get in the river to take the rope across so I can pull the net round. That's your job.'

I told uncle Buck I didn't fancy that. It was too cold for me. Poaching was a family business to him. I don't know why, but I guess one for the pot was a good saving on the housekeeping money. Rabbits, pheasants, salmon, trout, anything you wanted he'd get for you.

While we were filming in the middle of Kielder Forest we stumbled across a couple of young poachers on one of the north Tyne feeder streams. It was a pitch-black night in December and they were paddling up to their knees in icy water without waders. Neither seemed bothered that we had discovered them. There was no way we could identify them in the darkness and they knew the terrain well enough to escape much faster than we could chase them. What we saw was disturbing. The poachers were gaffing salmon after they'd spawned. Spent fish which offered no resistance when trapped in the glare of a motorbike headlamp. They caught two fish with their bare hands, flipping them on to the bank before diving on them and killing them. Nothing clever in that. We called across to them:

'Why take the risk for the sake of a five-pound salmon which isn't fit to eat anyway?'

'It's good fun. The police know everyone does it. If we get caught it's a fifteen hundred pound fine but no one will ever find us in the middle of the forest.'

The pair of them insisted they didn't poach to sell but said they'd consider it if someone offered them a lot of money. As for showing some regard for rod and line men who pay thousands of pounds for their sport, the poachers just laughed and said people like that must be 'mental'.

That's the thin end of a much bigger poaching wedge. The professionals have got it down to a fine art off the west coast of Ireland and on the big four salmon rivers of Scotland – the Tweed, Tay, Spey and Dee. On Deeside I witnessed some of the stock-in-trade of the big-time poacher. Robert Fettis runs a river-watch service for the Dee Fisheries and showed me a thirty-foot long trummel net he and his men had confiscated after a recent attack on a gang of four at Maryculter. They'd worked their way down a mile of river in their wet-suits, stretching the net across its width. All four got away in the chase. Robert was left with the multi-filament net and the five kelts plus two fresh fish inside it. Although the riverwatch team has night-sights and radio equipment, the dice are loaded in favour of the poaching gangs who descend on the Dee from all parts of Scotland as well as the north-east of England.

The most poached river in England must be the Wye, probably because of the number of towns along its route such as Hereford, Ross-on-Wye, Gloucester, Monmouth, etc. From the West Midlands it's only a short run down the M5. The Wye also has a reputation for big fish and a history of class struggles over the right to catch salmon, even as far back as the 1850s, when there sprang up a group of protesters called Rebeccaites who put on shawls and skirts to avoid identification when they took salmon from the Wye illegally.

The trouble over fishing rights started after a controversial act of Parliament removed all fishing rights from the common man and gave them to the crown. Only people with licences were allowed to fish. Naturally this deprived many country folk of part of their livings. There were riots in Rhayader in Wales and a policeman was actually killed. Eventually the fishing rights passed from the crown to private landowners, and they still remain in private ownership today.

The spirit of the Rebeccaites lives on as I saw by courtesy of the National Rivers Authority at Hereford. Out of their deep freeze they produced a magnificent thirty-six-pound cock salmon which had been seized from poachers in June. Such a great shame. There aren't too many of those in the Wye these days. It should have been left in the river to spawn or at least to be caught legitimately. That fish was worth about £100 at the fishmongers. The team of ghillies who confiscated it was led by a colourful character called George Woodward whose daughter, Lynn, is the only female ghillie in Britain. She had a hand in the operation too.

GEORGE AND DAUGHTER WITH A SALMON WHICH WASN'T POACHED

George, a Preston man who's gradually moved further and further south, told me the story of their successful night's policing.

'We were lucky and were in the right place at the right time. I picked up the night-sights for a routine check and couldn't believe my eyes. There was a dinghy coming across the river playing a net. I got in radio contact with the rest of the team on the other bank. We watched them lay four nets then moved in closer. Once they'd brought the dinghy off the river we rushed in. There was a bit of a chase and we found one of the poachers hiding in the undergrowth. He more or less confessed to everything. He showed us where they'd put the nets and we contacted the NRA bailiff and the police. The lad was a bit upset because he'd lost a lot of money. There were fifteen salmon in the net, the biggest thirty-six pounds, the smallest ten pounds. All those caught in less than an hour. Two of the poachers got away scot free but at least we apprehended one of 'em.'

Well done, George. It can't be much fun doing river surveillance all night when you've been working all day. The poacher's okay. He's probably unemployed – sleeping all day, poaching all night. I wondered if George had any sympathy.

'The chap who sneaks down to the river at night with a rod and line and takes a salmon for beer money, well, he's a nuisance but we can put up with him. It's the people who go out in organized gangs to commit wholesale slaughter I've no sympathy for whatsoever. Those are the sort of people who've plagued the Wye for the last six years. They don't sell the fish to boost the housekeeping – they blow it all in the pub.'

I could have spent all day listening to his tales of the Wye, which clearly he loved. I don't blame him. I wouldn't have a care in the world on a beat like Lydbrook. Of all the ghillies I met and spoke to during the writing of this book, George best summed up the attractions of the job:

'I've said to my boss many times, though *he*

THE WYE AT TINTERN. THE MOST PICTURESQUE SALMON RIVER IN THE WORLD – AND ONE OF THE MOST VULNERABLE

actually owns the stretch of river, it's *mine*. That's what hurts with the poaching. When you think of the hours you put in looking after *your* river, it's heartbreaking when someone comes and abuses it.'

There are two sides to every story, of course. The increased cost of salmon fishing, the fortunes made in recent years by timeshare operators and the fact that the river banks have virtually become no-go areas for the ordinary man have provoked the poacher even more. We persuaded a lifelong offender, Jim Edwards from Monmouth, to present the case for the defence. He showed absolutely no remorse. This is how the conversation went:

'Jim, I can understand you being a poacher because I used to poach as a kid with my uncle, but I gave it up because I wanted to be a footballer. What keeps you at it? Is it the money, the excitement, or both – or what?'

'There's no work so I'm looking for money. There's a little bit of excitement, I s'pose. I have to get psyched up first.'

'Where do you get rid of the fish?'

'Man in the street and hotels.'

'I thought they'd clamped down on hotels?'

'They're no problem.'

'Do you ever regret being a poacher?'

'No. We've got no town water other than Monmouth Bridge which is council-owned. That's only two hundred yards long and it's packed. Otherwise we have to pay two thousand pounds a year to fish a river we live on. The Duke of Beaufort owns our stretch. Our only hope is to go netting. I'm not going to make a fortune because I don't have a big fast car. Poaching's blown out of proportion.'

'Just a minute, Jim. Those people who pay two thousand pounds to fish a water that's already been emptied by you and your mates,

– don't you think they've a right to feel upset?'

'No, because the tidal water pushes fresh fish through on every tide. Tonight we could have twenty fish in a pool. By six o'clock in the morning they could be at Hay-on-Wye.'

'Unless you've netted 'em, you mean!'

'No, no, no. There are always fresh fish in the river.'

'How many times have you been caught?'

'Three.'

'What did you get?'

'I was let off once – no evidence. Then I got fined a hundred pounds and two years ago a thousand.'

'Could you pay it?'

'I have.'

'Out of poaching?'

'Yeah.'

'So it's a vicious circle?'

'Exactly.'

'What's next, gaol?'

'Could well be. Or a suspended sentence. The thousand-pound fine from Chepstow magistrates was a bit hard but if you've no work you've got to go back to the river to catch more salmon to pay your fine.'

'You could try getting a proper job instead.'

'What, in Monmouth?'

The more fishermen there are, the more jobs are created, ghillies, hotel staff, tackle manufacturers, etc., but the more the livelihoods of drift net fishermen at sea are threatened. Every year the cry to have the netsmen banned grows louder from the fishing fraternity. Ireland, England and Greenland are now the only places in Europe where drift netting is permitted. Even Japan is to ban it from 1993.

The Minister of Agriculture John Gummer has announced recently that drift net fishing off the English coast is to be phased out. It'll be a gradual process with the number of netting licences being reduced over a period of years. In a nutshell, the rod and line men blame the drop in the numbers of salmon coming into British rivers on the netsmen of Yorkshire and Northumberland. Ian Gregg, the chairman of the Tweed Commissioners put it this way:

'It's ridiculous, Jack, that every other country in the North Atlantic has banned nets at sea, and it's illegal in Scotland. How do you think Scottish fishermen feel when their rivers are depleted? They believe the fish heading for their rivers never get there.'

'But the drift nets are off at the end of August and the heavy runs of salmon don't happen until September, October and November.'

'No, that's not correct. There are large runs in the summer. The drift net fishery off the coast of Northumberland takes a declared fifty thousand salmon every year – grilse and mature fish. A lot of grilse do get through the mesh, but they're damaged.'

Surely it's understandable that people who take fish out at sea, and do it for a living, were entitled to their fair share of the money to be made from salmon. After all, a rod at the Tweed's Junction Pool costs £3,000 in a peak week.

'That's an argument put forward too often. There are very few beats like the Junction. There are plenty of Fords and only one or two Rolls Royces. The majority of fishing's done by ordinary people who are paying a reasonable price for their sport – about what you'd pay for a holiday in Majorca. The exclusiveness's exaggerated.'

To hear the drift net fishermen's justification of what they do, I spent a morning five miles off the coast of Amble with John Brown who'd been netting for a quarter of a century. He and 125 others pay £700 a year for a licence to fish. John's forked out around £2,000 before he starts, what with the £1,000 for the monofilament net and the upkeep of his boat. The net's the killer, literally. Anything can get tangled up in it and if it breaks loose from the boat it'll go on fishing forever more because it doesn't disintegrate. That's one of the main bones of contention. From the fisherman's

TOUGH WAY TO EARN A LIVING! A DRIFT NET FISHERMAN'S LOT IS NOT A HAPPY ONE. I FEEL FOR THEM

point of view it means he can go out in the daytime and not at night as he had to do with the old nylon nets. Sea fishing at night's a hazardous game! John reckons he was catching sixty to seventy salmon a day in the early 1980s. Now he's lucky if he gets fifteen. I think that's because they've overfished the sea, but I couldn't get him to agree.

I watched 600 yards of net slip into the water and after four hours bobbing about on a chilly sea, he'd caught one salmon. Seems to me there won't be any need to ban it at this rate. John works hard during the season – sixteen hours a day for five days a week between April and August. He was angry at talk of an international ban:

'You shouldn't stop someone's livelihood for someone else's pastime.'

His colleague, 'Ebb' Kenton was more forthcoming, though equally appalled at the attitude of the 'haves' towards the 'have-nots'.

'We average a thousand tonnes of salmon a year. Is that so detrimental to them? We're all in this world to make a living as best we can. Drift netting's a long-established tradition. If we don't salmon fish, what else do we do? It's an area of high unemployment. The mines are nearly all shut. Now they want to stop this.'

Ebb made out the best case for drift netting I've ever heard when he said that if you took away the licences it would be a free-for-all. Every Tom, Dick or Harry could be out there catching an unlimited amount of fish with an unlimited amount of net. He's right when he says the drift netters provide a lot of the policing themselves all year round because when they finish salmon netting in August they're out catching lobsters and shrimps and making sure no one's after salmon. In other words, it would be foolish to think that removing the nets would stop the practice because it would actually *increase* it, as it has in Scotland. A very interesting point I hadn't thought about before. Ebb was a good talker and we finished with a real ding-dong debate which ended just about honours even. I'll let you be the judge:

'Why is it wrong to drift net for salmon but all right to do it for mackerel or herring? A fish is a fish.'

'Yes but salmon are special —'

'They're emotive you mean!'

'— they begin and end in rivers.'

'And the landed gentry own the rivers.'

'No, no, don't blame the landed gentry —'

'It seems that might and money always has a swipe at the poor old underdog.'

'No, I've got a few bob and I fish a bit, but I've also got pals who like to think that when it's their turn there might be some fish in the river.'

'Obviously they've got the time and the money to do it.'

'They save up.'

'I can neither afford to save up nor take time to do it! Come on, Jack, we're all to blame to a degree, including anglers. Every fish going into a river is going to spawn. You catch 'em before they get a chance. Are you any less to blame for the drop in numbers?'

'We're selective. We put the hens back.'

'How many sportsmen do you know who put salmon back?'

'On the Tweed that's the policy.'

'That would be fine if all sportsmen did it but the first few caught up the Coquet here by sportsmen the other week were all weighed in at the fish market to cover the cost of licences. So they're *not* sportsmen!'

'With the numbers you seem to be catching I don't think it's going to be worth going offshore to fish.'

'I'm sure if someone gave us a lot of money we'd stop!'

The 'ordinary' man as we keep calling him still has a chance to fish for salmon even if he lives south of Yorkshire. A few put-and-take salmon fisheries have been set up around the country. I went to see one of the first in Britain at Ringstead Grange near Kettering in Northamptonshire. It was an absolute delight to have as my travelling companion Herbert Norton, a sharp-eyed and extremely well-bred eighty-six-year-old who remembered treading the platform at St Pancras Station as a six-year-

old. His grandfather, a wealthy stockbroker from Essex, used to take the family fishing and shooting to Scotland for three months at a time. St Pancras was the starting point of our journey to Ringstead. The Nortons' journey would begin a little further east. Let Herbert tell the tale:

'The route my grandfather took was unique. It's not possible today. He would hire a special train, two coaches pulled by a tank engine which used to collect us at Upminster station. The whole family embarked – father, mother, uncle, aunt, dogs, maids, the lot! The little train would bring us around the north of London to St Pancras to attach to the night sleeper to Scotland. Eventually we reached Brechin where we all piled into two horse-drawn waggonettes for the remaining four miles of a wonderfully exciting expedition.'

Lovely, isn't it, to think of that little tank engine chugging along with the maids and dogs? The funny thing is that Herbert's grandfather wasn't with them. He used to travel up with his good lady in a car driven by two chauffeurs, taking three days. He loved cars apparently. What style though. He and his son would spend all day shooting, then Herbert's father, who was much keener on the fishing, would dash down to the South Esk on his bike to catch a few fish before changing for dinner at the castle.

'Very formal then?' I asked Herbert.

'Oh yes. That's the way we lived, kedgeree on silver platters, Scotch beef and salmon. This persisted for a very long time. My wife and I always changed for dinner at home whether there was anyone there or not. She put on a short dress and I put on a dinner jacket.'

But how did Herbert's grandfather, not to mention his father, manage three months off work? Imagine trying to do it today!

'My grandfather made a great deal of money in the Australian gold mining boom around the turn of the century. He was a very skilful jobber and took full advantage.'

He must have done. It's a bit special when you hire your own train. As we approached

IN SHE GOES – OR IS IT A HE? TRIPLOID SALMON JOINS THE PUT-AND-TAKE TROUT AT RINGSTEAD

never otherwise have of catching a salmon. Having said that, there's been a good deal of criticism in the angling press about the stocking of trout lakes with salmon. The purists regard it as entertainment not sport and don't like the idea of someone catching a whopper of a salmon which has been farm reared, then claiming the British record. To be honest I can't see what the fuss is all about.

We arrived at the same time as a lorry load of triploids (sexless salmon) from a farm near the west coast of Scotland. They were corkers, each weighing ten to fifteen pounds. One by one we eased them into the lake. They laid in the margins for several minutes until they were acclimatized and then they were off possibly to give someone the thrill of a lifetime when he somehow got one on the end of his line.

Bob Nightingale, a tool fitter from the area, is one of Ringstead's most regular customers. He caught twenty-seven salmon there in 1990. And all for £10 a day with a bag limit of six fish.

Bob said, 'I can't think of anywhere where I could fish for that sort of money. I can do it right through the trout season for eleven months a year. You can learn the water and find out where the fish hold and with practice you can get quite proficient at catching them. The added advantage is that we know the salmon are always here.'

Too true. Actually knowing there are fish to catch can keep you fishing until the cows come home. The interesting thing about the triploids is that they keep up their weight by reverting to feeding in freshwater. They take shrimps off the bed of the lake. Not only that, they become strong fighting fish. As Bob said, the biggest problem can be getting a strong enough hook to stand up to them. He's had some salmon take eighty yards of line on their first run, jumping as they went!

Fred J. Taylor was there too. It was the first time I'd had a chance to speak to the legendary coarse angler and writer who was about to demonstrate another of his skills. Fred was

Kettering station on our way to showing Herbert the opposite end of the fishing spectrum, he told me that he still remembered the names of the ghillies from 1912. The head keeper was Bob and he had a son called Frank and a dog called Henry. The other keeper was Lyndsay. Blimey, I have trouble remembering the names of some of my players!

A short drive and we were at Ringstead which is a fishery stocked with 600 trout a week and forty salmon a month. It's a nice idea because it gives the locals a chance they'd

BOB NIGHTINGALE MAKES THE CASE FOR RINGSTEAD. THE ONLY CHANCE OF A SALMON FOR HIM AND THOUSANDS LIKE HIM

a baker in his early working days and as an out-and-out countryman has picked up loads of campfire cooking tips from around the world. Fred was going to cook us a fresh salmon from the lake in the style of the Irish ghillies on the great loughs. That consisted of wrapping the fish in several layers of soaking wet newspaper before putting it into the embers.

Herbert and I left him to it while we went fishing. He'd brought along his Castle Connell Greenheart rod, which he last used before going off to defeat Mr Hitler in 1939. The leather thongs he tied it with brought back boyhood memories for me. I used to nick the leather laces from my father's pit boots to put in my football boots. Herbert was adamant he wanted to put the rod into service again but it was a very windy day and I persuaded him to pack it away before it got damaged. Rods like that are for hanging on the wall and showing to people.

We fished from a boat and from the shore but had no luck. Herbert was terrific company. He conjured up images of a bygone age when sport really was available only to the privileged one per cent. I loved this story about his parents' honeymoon in 1904:

'Father took my mother fishing on the Inver in Scotland and got into a fish. He was on one bank, my mother on the other. Mother tried to bring the gaff across the stepping stones but the wind got up, caught her dress and in she went. Father's still playing the fish saying, 'You all right?' Unfortunately for him the road to Loch Inver runs along the river. A coach happened to be passing and drew up to see the fun. Word got back so that when father returned to the Stock Exchange a few weeks later there was a damned great notice up on the wall: "When you are playing a fish and your wife is drowning, which do you get out first? The fish, says Norton!"'

A typical fisherman's tale. Meanwhile Fred thought the salmon was ready and called us over for the unveiling ceremony. As he peeled off the paper, the skin came with it. Underneath, the flesh was cooked to perfection.

Fred joked:

'How the poor live!' He continued: 'Jack, you've been on the Tay, the Dee and the Spey but I bet you didn't get better than this.'

He was dead right. We must have looked an odd trio as we sat by the ashes of the fire on the shores of the lake eating bread and chunks of salmon with our bare hands.

HERBERT NORTON AND HIS CASTLE CONNELL GREENHEART.
FISHING FOR LAKE SALMON — A NEW EXPERIENCE FOR HIM

'It just goes to show you don't have to be a millionaire to catch salmon or to eat it,' said Fred.

I asked Herbert what he thought of the lake.

'A lovely place. Gives a lot of people a chance to fish for salmon who otherwise couldn't do it. We had a pull out there, Jack, but I think it was a trout.'

We ended the day with a glass of wine, more salmon and Herbert considering the prospect of the Thames being revived as a salmon fishery. Work has been going on for several years now, installing passes in the weirs so the fish can get upstream to spawn. Although the Thames is close to his home, he wasn't at all keen on the idea. We'll leave the last word to Herbert Norton, stockjobber, raconteur and bon viveur, slumming it for a day with Fred and me:

'If you were to introduce, as would be possible, a really big run of salmon into the Thames again then all the people with money would buy up stretches of river and reserve areas for themselves. Hundreds of thousands of coarse fishermen would be debarred. That can't be right.'

FISHERMAN, RACONTEUR AND CHEF. FRED J. TAYLOR'S MOST AT HOME BY THE CAMPFIRE

CHAPTER TWO

VIKING LINE

Every summer there's an exodus of Geordies to Bergen and Trondheim in Norway. They go to fish great rivers like the Vosso and the Orkla but sad to report neither of them is producing as many catches as they were in the 1980s. Even so, the salmon there are a darned sight more plentiful than in my local river, the Tyne. That's not really surprising when you think how filthy the rivers were when it was an industrial area. With the mines, steelworks, shipyards and ICI all going strong in the north-east, salmon had a poor time of it.

Slowly the rivers are improving but you shouldn't get too excited when people tell you they've spotted a salmon in the Wear. There's always the odd salmon or two. They've begun restocking the Wear, as they have the Thames west of London, but you can't just re-create a salmon river overnight, so to say. It takes a lot of time to create the right conditions.

The Tyne's in better shape. Now the big industries have gone, the water's a lot cleaner and it's become the premier salmon river in England, outstripping the Wye, a good proportion of which is in Wales anyway. The Kielder Hatchery is the cause of the increase in fish stocks. When the creation of the Kielder water reservoir was proposed, to supply water to the big north-east community, the riparian landowners and angling associations kicked up a fuss. They wouldn't agree to a dam unless a hatchery or a fish ladder was installed. Since it was doubtful that salmon would be fit enough to tackle a ladder 172 feet high (the height of the dam), especially when they had already been in freshwater for up to nine months, a hatchery it was.

In 1978 salmon were almost extinct in the Tyne. It still has five times as many sea trout as salmon, but thanks to Peter Gray and his work at Kielder, salmon stocks have been considerably improved. By 1978 only a measly thirty fish were caught a season on average. By 1991 the figure had shot up to 2,000. I've fished the river quite a lot and there's no doubt it fishes well in certain parts. It's shallow and there aren't that many good holding places, but Tyne salmon seem to be good takers. Fishermen get a good return for the number of fish in the river.

What goes on at the hatchery is fascinating. At the back end of the year, Peter and his men sweep parts of the north and south Tyne and the river Rede with their electro-nets. The top end of the north Tyne's been lost as a spawning area because of the dam and to compensate the angling clubs and river owners Peter has to put back each year 160,000 of the parr spawned (artificially if you like) at Kielder. Since the hatchery started in 1978, they have in fact returned twice that number of fish. Now they're restocking the Coquet, Wear and Tees. I went out with the Kielder team on a freezing day in early December when the last of the salmon were being stunned in the river. I was full of admiration for what they do but I put it to Peter that it was a bit unnatural to take salmon from one river and try to introduce them into another. His view was a practical one:

'That's all right if you've got plenty of salmon in these other rivers but we make no pretence about what we're doing – trying to re-establish fish in rivers where they've become scarce. Any salmon's better than no salmon at all. In any case we've proved here by micro-tagging that fish return to the river we've put them in and not to the river where they were born.'

I watched the team take a dozen or so salmon in the electro-nets. If these fish had spawned in the river most of the eggs would have been lost because the water temperature from the reservoir is too warm during the winter. The salmon are only semi-stunned then taken back to the hatchery to be stripped of their eggs, which is an amazing process.

The salmon in the hatchery tanks weighed anything up to seventeen or eighteen pounds but seemed to be under stress. Peter assured me that everything was okay because they'd be stressed in the river at spawning time anyway, when the males get very aggressive with each other, which raises a very interesting point. When salmon are paired in the wild, according to Peter, it's one hen to one cock. At the hatchery one cock's capable of fertilizing about six large females. It would be daft to try it though because there could be a problem with the milt from that particular cock. Normally they use two or three cocks to six hens.

Stripping the eggs is an expert job so I declined Peter's invitation to have a go and settled instead for a support role. On went the plastic apron and I helped him lift the first hen out of the bucket. I couldn't help wondering if this was the only way the salmon would survive all the pressures we're placing on it. Just imagine if there was a mammal higher up the food chain than us which farmed human beings at a hatchery and decided what the population of Northumberland would be.

Applying pressure along the fish's belly, Peter made the eggs pour into the bowl at a phenomenal rate. A hen weighing about twelve pounds was reduced to three-quarters of that in a few minutes.

'Bloody hell,' I couldn't help exclaiming, 'she's full to bursting.'

'Aye, a good number there. This one'll go

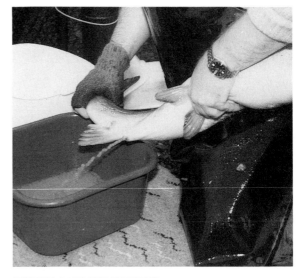

STRIPPING A HEN FISH AT KIELDER

back on Monday tagged. She'll be over twenty pounds if she comes back in a couple of years. It's a kelt now and not worth eating.'

He emptied another hen of its eggs before picking the right male. One of them, a big one, wouldn't produce much sperm so it was returned to the tank.

'Big isn't always best,' said Peter.

The next one was better. Quite a sight to see the white milt splashing all over the eggs. Kielder salmon produce around a million eggs a year from which Peter reckons to get about 600,000 fish. The eggs go into the hatchery until the following March and a week *before* they're due to hatch they go back into the river having been protected from the hazards in the wild, things like predators, poachers and winter floods.

'You mean you actually put *eggs* back in the river?' I asked Peter.

'Yes, we have to. We can hold two million in the hatchery, but we've only got facilities for rearing six hundred thousand fish.'

Next came the fertilization process, a simple business of adding water to the eggs and milt. Within thirty seconds there's near enough 100 per cent fertility because all the material's confined to the bowl. (In fast water on natural streams a lot of the milt gets washed away.)

SOFTLY, SOFTLY. ONE FALSE MOVE AND THEY ARE DEAD

That done, the contents of the bowl are washed and drained to get rid of any dead sperm then the eggs are put into baskets. After that it's a case of wait and hope. This is the way Peter describes it:

'Next spring, when the water temperature comes up to forty-six degrees Fahrenheit, they'll start to hatch. Normally it takes between a hundred and sixty and a hundred and eighty days for eggs to hatch up here but that's nature being clever because if they hatch too quickly the little fish won't find the food they need until the water temperature gets up to fifty degrees Fahrenheit.'

They keep a very close watch on the eggs once they're in the tanks. With something like 25,000 eggs in a basket, each potentially worth £1,000, you can appreciate why. The baskets are checked twice a day to remove any that are turning white. It's essential to avoid noise and vibration. Bang your hand against the side of the tank and thousands of pounds' worth of potential fish die. Peter explained:

'They are the most delicate things you could imagine between fertilization and what we call the eyed-ova stage. Once you see those two little black eyes and the fish have started to form a backbone they become exactly the opposite – very tough.'

Back outside we went for more fertilization and to study the different shapes of cock and hen fish. I pulled a fifteen pounder out of the bucket and laid it on the table while Peter, the expert, told me all about kypes and adipose fins. The kype or gib on the bottom jaw is the main difference between males and females. The male salmon grows it during the spawning season. If the salmon survives and gets back to the sea, the kype will disappear again, absorbed into the body. On top of that, the cock fish is sleeker and more flat-sided than the hen especially when she's full of eggs.

Now to the adipose fin. That's the small fin between the dorsal and the tail. Rod fishermen in the Tyne area should look out for salmon with the adipose missing. That's a sign that it might have a micro-tag implanted in its nose. The fin's amputated under anaesthetic when the fish is juvenile. Peter showed me a hen salmon with the adipose removed. What we were looking at was one of the Kielder salmon having returned home.

'If we're lucky the tag'll still be in the nose,' said Peter. 'When we've recovered it I can tell you the day, the month and the year that we released the fish from the hatchery. I can tell you whether we released it in the Rede, the north Tyne, south Tyne or main Tyne. We can be as accurate as that. Every single fish has returned to the spot where it was put in the river. Not a single mistake. We've had tags returned from the west coast of Greenland, Ireland, the Faroes and the east coast of Scotland.'

It's only recently that we've discovered more about the migratory routes of this mysterious fish. When nuclear submarines went under the polar ice cap off the coast of Greenland they found vast shoals of salmon on their radar. Before that we could only guess what the salmon got up to at sea and where on earth their feeding grounds were. Now the Canadians are keeping an eye out for tagged fish from Kielder. If they see the UK code, the tags are returned to the Ministry of Agriculture who in turn let Peter and his team know. Peter was anxious to reassure those anglers who are worried about micro-tagging:

'The project isn't to stop people catching salmon. We just want to know who's catching how many and where, so that the fisheries can be properly managed.'

That sounds sensible to me.

The hen with the missing adipose was duly stripped of her eggs – about 10,000 we estimated. It left her with a huge empty sac under her belly as you can imagine. Strange, all that salmon roe and nobody eats it on this side of the world. In fact it's illegal to have it in your possession in the UK. I must say I might enter the league of fishermen who believe in putting hens back after watching what goes on at Kielder. It's a sad occasion when you catch a nice big hen fish and cut her up at home only to find she's full of eggs. I always feel a tinge of sadness. Peter said:

'What a lot of people don't understand is that a salmon can come along in February and March and be in the river for a few months waiting to spawn. When they catch a spring fish there's no weight in it. The salmon, as we know, eat nothing in freshwater. In a river like the Tweed, which contains thousands of fish averaging ten pounds in weight, there isn't the food supply for them anyway. So the hen will produce eggs from her own body fat, and the flesh goes a dirty grey colour because all the protein has gone into the eggs. The food value is nil. All she wants to do is go back into the river and then to the sea to recover. If we're lucky she'll come back twice the size.'

I couldn't leave the hatchery without holding a handful of fingerlings. Wonderful sensation. Such beautiful little fish. They'd had the meals on wheels service for the last twelve months and ninety per cent had survived from the eggs stripped last year. I wanted Peter to dump a few of them in my garden pond but he wouldn't hear of it!

Peter took me to watch nature's own version of what goes on at the hatchery just a few miles away along the north Tyne. I thought we wouldn't have a ghost of a chance of seeing salmon spawning in the river but he seemed confident. I had to swear not to identify the precise part of the river. The sun was dropping fast but the air was clear and cold and the river had a faint orange tinge to it. It was a perfect spot to stand and watch and there wasn't another soul around. Over on the far side was a whole stack of fish squabbling and splashing in shallow water. I'd never seen anything like it on a Northumberland river. The future generation of fish for Tyne anglers was being started before our eyes. We could almost see the females scoop out holes in the gravel to deposit their eggs. The males lie close behind ready to release their sperm. The hen then moves a few feet upstream and cuts another hole. The gravel she excavates is carried downstream to cover the fertilised eggs in the first hole. There was a real kerfuffle when a cock appeared uninvited and the other cocks tried to drive the intruder away. If we'd been in Canada they'd have had a place like this roped off and a viewing platform for the public installed.

Cock salmon are funny creatures. The hens back off after finishing their work and head for the sea but the males linger on the redds sometimes for another two months. The mating instinct then causes them to fight for possession of more females, which eventually takes a heavy toll of them because the fights often cost the cocks their lives. Even though they won't have eaten for ten months they're so desperate they keep going till they drop.

The next time I crossed the Tyne it was midsummer and I was on the way to pick up a flight from Newcastle to Trondheim. Midsummer is when those rod men who can afford it head for Norway. The famous river Vosso was having a hard time so our destination was the Orkla, reckoned to be the third most productive salmon river in the country. Opening day three weeks earlier had seen some terrific catches so we were looking forward to good sport. I was also looking

THE VOSSO IS NORWAY'S LEADING SALMON RIVER BUT THINGS AREN'T WHAT THEY WERE

forward to meeting one of the acknowledged world experts on salmon fishing, Arthur Oglesby from Harrogate, who was already fishing at Svorkmo only a mile or so from the lodge where we'd be staying.

As we drove around the bay at Orkhanger, the nearest town, I was disappointed to see diamond nets all up the fjord. Obviously the fishermen knew the favourite salmon runs and staked out their nets accordingly. They must take an enormous quantity of fish through the season. I saw one of them in his boat about 200 yards offshore checking the net as they do there every so often during the day, but he didn't have a catch. It didn't augur well.

But as we crossed the Orkla a few miles further on there was a sight to cheer me up: caravans along the shore and a couple of dozen rod and line men enjoying themselves on a lovely fast-running stretch of water. It was a ticket water that cost 150 kroner (£14) a day, which is quite cheap for such a good river.

It was the sort of place I'd love to fish for a week, casting from the shore or the gravel island with no one to bother you and the chance to fish all through the night if you wanted to, with help from the couple of bottles of whisky in the caravan. That would just suit me. One of the men said twenty fish had been taken the previous day so maybe the diamond netters weren't so clever after all.

Our lodge was owned by Lief Gundersruud, an Oslo businessman who loved his fishing. He tried to spend as much time as he could there during the summer because it's a very short season, May to August. In early autumn it starts to get dark and very cold and then he shuts the lodge until next summer. Lief didn't speak much English and although the Geordie dialect has something in common with Norwegian, understanding each other wasn't that easy. It was 8 p.m. Time to find Arthur while he was still on the river.

On the way we passed a little pile of stones with a bunch of flowers in it on a very nasty bend. Somebody must have had a dreadful crash judging by the tyre marks. Drunken driving is a major problem in Norway where people find the long winter days depressing. People are allowed to buy stills and make their own form of whisky. Alcoholism is rampant. 'In summer we fish and make love,' they say. 'In winter we don't fish!' We were to hear more about those flowers by the roadside.

We found the bridge at Svorkmo where Arthur said he'd be fishing. He was pleased to see us and I could tell we'd get on well. Just watching him Spey cast in midstream was an education. He had a lovely fluid movement that contained no apparent effort. Unfortunately even the maestro was having no luck. Arthur had caught a nice twenty-nine-pound fish the day before but there didn't seem to be any in the river today. All the usual theories were put forward: drift netting in the estuary; acid rain; too many sportsmen. Arthur thought this pretty little pool was our best bet. The ice on the mountains melts at midsummer, the river rises and the salmon run in.

Last year they'd been everywhere. Maybe we were late. Maybe they'd already gone way upstream. Who could tell?

'I've never had a fish out of this pool but I've lost them here,' Arthur said. 'If there are any at all they should be here but they're scarce and becoming scarcer, which is the case almost everywhere you go.'

He was using an intermediate line to get the fly down in the water but he thought a fish had to take within the next half a dozen casts or it wouldn't take at all that evening. He ought to know. He'd been fishing in Norway for thirty years having been attracted by the lure of the big fish, the chance of catching a forty to fifty pounder. In fact he'd had four of more than forty pounds, the heaviest weighing in at forty-six and a half. This is how he told it:

'Ever since I was a small boy I've been fascinated by moving water. A lot of men are hunters at heart but it's one thing hunting above ground where you can see your quarry and quite another hunting underwater. Water has a magic about it. You never know what's beneath the surface. It could be a six-inch trout or a forty-pound salmon.'

Those are exactly my views. I find just being beside water can be thrilling. You don't have to fish to feel the magic. I get great fulfilment out of watching its changing moods and the way water changes colour with the sky. When I was a kid up in Northumberland, rivers were exciting things to come across. Wherever there's water there's wildlife. I used to think nothing of setting off across the hills for the day on some safari or other, walking miles, stopping to sit by the edges of streams and dropping in unannounced on one of my aunties expecting her to provide me with something to eat. They always did because families were close in the 1940s.

Arthur told me how the behaviour of cows used to help him on his fishing adventures. He reckoned if there were cattle lying in a field nearby he'd come out of the water for a rest, but if they got up and started chomping from

Spring salmon fishing is not what it was but Low Church pool on the magnificent river Spey is one of the best

I never thought I'd get a chance to fish on the Royal estate at Balmoral! The Queen has three boats on the Dee and thanks to a Cheshire businessman I had half an hour's casting in early April. Fancy being able to tell your friends that!

Visiting Kielder Hatchery is a real education. Peter Gray and his men are doing some marvellous work breeding salmon in captivity. 160,000 parr are returned to north-east rivers each year

Don't believe people who tell you that man-made reservoirs ruin the environment. Kielder water near where I live is not only beautiful but has indirectly improved salmon catches on the Tyne

Norway's river Orkla has a history of producing big fish in midsummer when the snows have melted
I shouldn't be doing this! 'Burning the water' on the Tweed is poaching when all's said and done

one end of the field to the other he felt it was time to get back in the water. There's a tip for you. There weren't any cows near the Orkla but if there had been they'd have been lying down. Nothing doing. Arthur and his colleagues decided to call it a day. We followed them up the hillside to their lodge for a wee dram and a bit of après-fish. It was already ten o'clock at night but you would never have noticed. In summer it hardly gets dark that far north.

I was interested to hear Arthur's views on the Kielder Hatchery. He disliked fish farming for commercial reasons as much as I do but I had come to see the value of what Peter was doing on the Tyne. Did Mr Oglesby agree?

'Man meddles a lot in my opinion. When he picks up a hen fish and strips the eggs from it, then covers those eggs with milt from a cock of his choice, who's to say those two fish would have selected each other as partners in the wild? We assume too much. All right, we're putting fish back into the rivers but we don't know how we're disturbing the genetic side. The future's bleak, I think. Old people tend to say that, I know, and they talk about the good old days, but the fact is I used to catch a hundred and fifty to a hundred and sixty fish a year and now I'm lucky to get into double figures.'

Before we knew it, five of us had emptied a large bottle of malt while exchanging salmon tales. It doesn't matter how many hours you talk, you always learn something new. By now it was already daylight, the sun having hardly dipped below the horizon. We needed headlights on the car but only as a safety precaution. Getting to sleep in daylight's no problem with a few glasses inside you.

Next morning I had a casting lesson with the maestro. He's tutored a few characters in his time. One of them was a feller he nicknamed Frobisher. All he was interested in was getting stoned, according to Arthur. Nothing wrong with that but poor old Frobisher was so incapable when the time came to fish that he'd frequently fall in.

Like Arthur, I've heard tales of monster fish being caught in Norwegian rivers. The British pioneered sport fishing here, reminding the locals of the tremendous natural resources they had. There's the story of Mr Wells, an old master at Eton, who, on his eightieth birthday, caught his eightieth salmon of forty pounds or more. Fish of that size were once reasonably commonplace. While Arthur was urging me to give my casting 'a bit more umpty' he told me his attitude to big fish had changed.

'It was in the mid-sixties when I caught my forty-six and a half pounder. What a milestone. It came at an enthusiastic moment in my life. It happened on the river Vosso on the night of my arrival and I was fortunate enough to have a young cameraman with me. He filmed it pretty well. I even had black hair in those days. Now I've lost the urge to catch another big fish. I prefer to take on a challenging bit of water and worry about the weight of the fish afterwards.'

Standing up to our thighs in water on a cool, grey day with not a hope of catching a fish wasn't the most rewarding way of spending a morning. I must confess I get a little bored when I don't catch sight of a salmon. Lovely clear water though, surrounded by bright green hillsides with the odd timber building in red or yellow dotted about. Norway is so silent. Apart from the sound of the water there was nothing. I lit up a cigar and began to think about fishing and football. People ask me if I get excited at football matches and I say no. I remain cool so I can assess what's going on. Don't get me wrong, I still get angry, like when we tossed away goals in the last fifteen minutes in our European Championship qualifier in Poland, but excitement doesn't come into it. Very often my mind will drift off. I'll be wishing I was on the riverbank instead of standing by the dug-out.

A good friend of mine, Jock Stein, died at a match. I won't but I might die floating down a river with a salmon on! Salmon generate that sort of excitement. Look at their life cycle. They're born in the river where they have to

ARTHUR OGLESBY HAS A TREMENDOUS RECORD IN NORWAY.
HE GAVE ME A FEW PRICELESS TIPS

scratch around for every morsel they can find. Then nature gives them a silvery coat and tells them it's time to go to sea through all the filth and pollution we've allowed to collect in British rivers. Somehow they get through that, then begins the enormous journey under the Arctic ice Peter talked about. Nature then demands they come back to the river they were born in to start the cycle all over again. Of course the most peculiar thing of all is that they don't feed once they're in the river so why do we stand there for hours on end trying to persuade them to take a fly? Arthur has a theory about this:

'I liken salmon to a half-sleeping cat by the back door when a leaf flutters past. Sometimes the cat will dab at the leaf with its paw and play with it. It knows the leaf isn't edible but it has triggered off a predatory reflex action. Salmon are much the same. They don't need the fly as food but it sparks off a memory of their rich sea-feeding days. Creatures that hunt have to stay in practice.'

Creatures that eat have to stay in practice too. It was lunchtime and my stomach was rumbling. Our hosts couldn't provide any salmon but they certainly fed us well, with a whole chicken, boiled potatoes and peas washed down with several glasses of beer.

'What's happened to the fish?' I asked Lief.

'They'll be here tonight. There are fish in the river already. Last year five thousand salmon.'

I wasn't too bothered about last year. A fellow guest, Erik, whose sons had caught a couple of thirty-pound fish on opening day, showed me the lure they planned to use, a Rapala. I'd seen them before, a small imitation fish which spins and sinks. Around Lief's lodge there were some marvellous old photographs of Edwardian gentlemen holding up giant salmon; and one dated 1969 which showed Prince Philip and his Norwegian ghillie in a boat. So the Duke had been here too, eh? I wonder if he caught anything. To tell you the truth, I wasn't aware that he went salmon fishing.

While we rested after lunch, Lief put on a video about the art of Spey casting with Leonard Parkin, the former ITN newscaster, providing the commentary, and blow me there was Arthur Oglesby. It was subtitled in Norwegian. Hope they got their royalties. Lief also showed me a home-made video of the opening-day catches – and he was right. The salmon were leaping everywhere. Lief was so confident of success on his beat that night that I felt sure we were in for a productive session. First though I needed to change some money to tip the ghillies and stand a few drinks at the bar.

Walking down the main street I was struck by how quiet it was. Not a soul about. The bank was shut although the sign seemed to say it should be open. There was one person in the adjoining office who explained that everything was closed. The whole village had gone to the funeral of a young couple killed in a car crash. Apparently they'd been hit by a drunken driver on the bend where we saw the flowers.

We joined Lief and company on a wide sweep of the Orkla with views over open countryside one way and a huge wall of granite on the other side. It was just like being in Scotland. It was twenty past midnight when we started to fish. A strange sensation. Normally by that time I'd have had a few pints and been well wrapped up in bed. They said it was the best time to fish and we planned to go on till 2 a.m. at least. I was quite enjoying it until I realized half an hour had gone by and there'd been no sign of salmon.

'It's okay,' said Lief. 'They'll be here soon.'

I didn't know whether he was genuinely optimistic or just trying to keep our spirits up. Three of us – Lief, me and the waitress from the lodge, whom I'll call Grunhilda because I couldn't pronounce her real name – kept working the same bit of water again and again. Grunhilda was about fifty years old, slim, blonde, attractive and divorced. She'd been introduced to salmon fishing three years before. The water was almost up to her armpits but she was quite happy to cast the night away. How many fish had she caught in three years I wondered?

'Five or six. Last year I catch five.'

'And this year?'

'One fish but not big. Last week I lost fish big as this,' she said stretching her hands about a yard apart. 'People look at me and they say "wow!" but I lost him and I cry a little bit.'

I reminded her about pheromones (more about them in Chapter 6) and told her always to dip her hand in the water so the body oils in her skin might attract fish.

'I'll do that.'

'Do the fishermen chase you?'

'No. I chase them. I like to be free woman, to go fishing when I want.'

'My wife doesn't much like me going fishing. She says I don't spend enough time at home.'

Then we walked off towards the bank to start a camp fire. It was getting chilly.

'It's sad,' said Grunhilda, 'no fish today.'

So ended my first excursion on the Orkla. A lot of conversation, some lovely company but not a hint of salmon. We sat around the crackling log fire watching a mink scurry down the far bank. Perhaps he knew something we didn't. It was 1.45 a.m. but it didn't matter. The sky was a breathtaking mixture of yellow, orange and blue and the crack was good. See you again, Norway.

CHAPTER THREE

UP THE
JUNCTION

The Tweed is a magical river. I first discovered it when I was a young pro at Leeds United. It was always out of my reach to fish but I was happy to sit and watch. Running water has that sort of fascination for me. I would take my daughter Debbie up to Melrose then across each of the bridges, zigzagging our way back to Berwick, before driving home to Newcastle. The round trip took a full day.

We lingered longest at the Junction Pool in Kelso where the Teviot joins the main Tweed because you could always see boats there and someone down the bank. It's a wonderful place just to sit and look and it's remarkable how many people come and sit beside you to talk fishing or football or to say nothing at all. There's so much to see. Apart from the salmon, which leap about everywhere in the autumn, there's usually a pheasant or a partridge overhead. I've stood under Kelso bridge many times and watched cormorants coming up out of the water with eels flopping out of their mouths. You'd see their throats bulging as they swallowed the eels whole.

This time I went back to the Junction at prime time in early November. It was a clear autumn day with just a touch of sharpness in the air. Kelso was at its best. Sir Walter Scott, the nineteenth-century novelist described it as 'the most beautiful village in Scotland'. I don't know that I go along with that but it's certainly my kind of border town – cobbled

square with Georgian buildings and lots of nooks and crannies to explore. Kelso also has the most unusual abbey I've ever seen. High up in the walls there are arrow slits indicating that it must have doubled as a fortress during the Border Wars, in which were fought some of the most violent battles the world has ever known. When I was a lad I had books chronicling the deeds of Rob Roy and his colleagues. The Tweed ran red with blood in medieval times. How different it was that bright November morning: gin-clear water full of fresh run salmon. In the space of a couple of minutes I saw half a dozen fish. Multiply that by twenty, they say, and you have some idea of how many there are in any particular section of the pool.

The lucky party fishing when I was there comprised Jim Miller, the chairman of a big UK corporation called the Harris Sheldon Group, which owns the pool, and his guests, including the financier Jim Slater who helped to pioneer timeshare fishing. We'd bump into them later. First I had the chance to do something I always wanted to do, that is take a helicopter ride along the Tweed. The weather couldn't have been better. From 300 feet the trees were an eye-catching mixture of green, brown and gold. The river threaded between them like a dark blue ribbon.

We set off downstream from Kelso. The first point of interest was Jeffreys Pool and Jeffreys Island which were the focus of a High Court dispute in March 1990. Jennifer Lovett from

Wark Farm on the south (English) bank of the Tweed claimed that anglers from a consortium on the north bank were trespassing over the centre line. History was on the lady's side and the latest Ordnance Survey map showed that the centre line in fact ran to the north of Jeffreys Pool. The judge, Mr Justice Mummery, decided Ms Lovett owned the salmon fishing rights in the pool.

Ahead of us I could just make out another famous border town, Coldstream, which used to be one of the cross-over points for runaway couples escaping to Scotland to get married. For me it has very different connections. There's a section of river called The Leys which I fished many times as I got older and better known. Below us was a man fishing in a boat just down from the weir where I used to go. It's one of the most exclusive beats on the Tweed but I never caught a thing there. Only a few hundred yards further along is the famous Coldstream Bridge. I remember an occasion in the late 1980s, when there was low water and the salmon were holding up there, when you couldn't get a place on the bridge

for sightseers. For a time Coldstream became a major tourist attraction. The fish were side by side all the way down the river.

It's noticeable on this part of the Tweed how fishermen tether themselves to the bank with a length of stout rope. It saves them having a ghillie and it means they can lower themselves down the river until the rope runs out, fishing perfectly safely on their own.

My fondest memory of the Tweed concerns the bridge at Norham village where I caught my biggest ever Atlantic salmon. It weighed twenty-eight and a half pounds. I was standing on a parapet under the bridge when I hooked him, but I was 300 yards down the river when I finally landed him. The struggle started quietly enough but by the time it was nearing its end there were twenty people on the bank enjoying the spectacle. Two guys ran into the water to net the salmon for me and bring it to the bank. They were soaked up to their waists, but I don't think they realized they were so excited. I bought a watercolour of the bridge to commemorate the occasion, not a very good one. It cost me £50.

KELSO WAS DESCRIBED BY SIR WALTER SCOTT AS THE PRETTIEST VILLAGE IN SCOTLAND. IT'S CERTAINLY MY KIND OF TOWN

AH! THE MEMORIES. THE BRIDGE AT NORHAM WHERE I CAUGHT MY BIGGEST ATLANTIC SALMON – 28½ LBS

Flying in low with the sun coming at us from the sea and the light catching the top of the water really showed Berwick at its best. It's a lovely little town. Three bridges span the river, one old, one very old and one very, very old. There can't be many places with more chequered histories either. Berwick changed its nationality four times, swinging between Scotland and England like a pendulum. It's firmly in England now but the people feel very independent. I heard Berwick even struck up its own private charter with the Soviet Union during Brezhnev's time.

From the salmon fishing point of view, this is a problem area for two reasons. The first is that there is river netting in the estuary, which is perfectly legal and above board, and the second is poaching, which certainly isn't. We landed by the estuary to find out more about netting. There was nobody better to tell us than Ralph Holmes whose family have owned netting stations here for 200 years. In the 1960s they had twenty stations but now it's

down to five. That's typical of what's been happening here. In order to preserve salmon for the rod and line man, the Atlantic Salmon Conservation Trust has bought out most of the twenty-seven netting stations.

At the turn of the century, Ralph's family would think nothing of catching 500 salmon with each tide. Now, in a good year, they're happy with 2,000 overall. There's an awful lot of argument over this method of fishing but Ralph puts up a very plausible case:

'We fish from mid-April to mid-September and depend for our living on a cycle of nine tides, each lasting four hours. Our fishing effort therefore is not that much. We catch ten to twenty per cent of the salmon in the river during those five months. It allows a lot of time for the fish to swim up the river system. The anglers get a good crack of the whip because in the autumn salmon are free to run through and spawn. That way we are assured of having a continuation of fish.'

Ian Gregg, the chairman of the Tweed

Commissioners, who insists that the estuary netters take most of the summer fish which are vital for sport, put the other side of the story.

'The few miles of Tweed from the estuary upwards was under more netting pressure than any river in Britain until most of the stations were bought. Even so there's still a significant presence in the estuary.'

As a fisherman I naturally sympathize with Ian's side of the argument. The fact is though that the net and cobble fishing, as they call it, has been going on at the mouth since the 1300s. The netsmen don't have an unlimited licence to print money either. One of the fisheries attracted an annual rent of 68 shillings and 8 pence in the early part of the century. Fifty years later the rent was down to 20 shillings because the numbers of fish had fallen away so badly. And this isn't sport we're talking about, it's a livelihood.

Ralph summed up his feelings this way. 'I never want to take too many fish. I've got two small boys and I want them to have salmon in the Tweed as well – and everyone else. I hope this river will still be good for fishing – and netting – for the next two thousand years.'

Poachers are rampant on the Tweed. During the drought years of 1989 and 1990 they had so many poachers in this part of the river that every ghillie from Newcastle to Edinburgh was called in to police the water around Berwick in the evening. It's a very difficult river on which to get a prosecution. You can find a poacher's net and lie in wait but unless you catch someone actually taking salmon out of it, they can say, 'It doesn't belong to me'. One of the ghillies told me that in one year alone they took 1,400 illegal nets from the Tweed, mostly in the estuary. And they aren't necessarily 100 feet long. They can be as basic as a garden net held down by stones and bottles. Poaching has become almost a national pastime.

Having heard the river netter's point of view we jumped aboard the helicopter again and flew twenty or so miles inland to Kelso. The first four and a half miles of the journey are in England and the next nineteen follow the English–Scottish border during which the Tweed, alone among British rivers, has dual nationality. The remaining seventy-five miles up to the source at Tweeds Wells are entirely Scottish. Because of its uniqueness, the river's

THIS MUST BE THE BEST SALMON BEAT IN THE WORLD – THE JUNCTION POOL WHERE THE TEVIOT MEETS THE TWEED

FLOORS CASTLE OWNED BY THE DUKE OF ROXBURGHE. I HOPE THE BEATS DON'T GET SPOILED BY TIMESHARE

managed by the Tweed Commissioners, a body set up by Act of Parliament. It's a big set-up with eighty members elected either by the various district councils or the river owners.

The Commissioners draw a levy of £25 for every fish caught in the river. Two-thirds of the money goes towards protecting the river – things like bailiffs – and a third towards scientific studies of one sort or another. For instance, the Tweed has a full-time biologist based at Melrose. It's his job to tag fish and monitor their migratory pattern.

With the sun behind us the Junction Pool looked splendid. As far as I'm concerned it's the most famous salmon pool in the world. Obviously it gets its name because of where it is, at the junction of the Tweed and the Teviot, which comes in from the south. The fish hold up here just below the weir. Whether it is to have a rest or gather their strength before tackling the weir and the salmon pass, who knows? It's certainly a prolific salmon pool. I'd only fished it once, with Ian Botham. We caught nothing but then it wasn't a peak week

like this. We came in to land over Floors Castle next door – the largest inhabited house in Great Britain with a window for each day of the year. Floors is owned by the Duke of Roxburghe who was just putting his beats, Upper and Lower Floors, up for timeshare. Quite expensive too. For a week in the high season he wanted £80,000; for a bad week £20,000. I once landed a fish on Lower Floors. A lovely clean fourteen-pound salmon in the height of summer when no one else was catching.

There to meet us on the lawns of the Ednam House Hotel was Alistair Brooks, the owner. This is what you call a traditional old fisherman's hotel, which owes its existence to the Junction Pool. September, October and November are frantic. That's why the Ednam House closes over Christmas and the New Year when most Scottish hotels expect to do their best business. It was started by Alistair's grandfather in 1932 and it's now passed down to the fourth generation of the family. 'It's not really a hotel,' he says, 'more like a club which

ALL ABOARD FOR MY TRIP DOWN THE TWEED

changes membership every week.' The same people come for the same week year in, year out.

We drove out of Kelso, through a farm gate, and headed for Jim Miller's fishing hut. The party were all out on the Junction, which stretches for about half a mile from the weir to beyond the main road bridge into town. I wandered down to the very point of the headland where the rivers meet. In front of me, in pole position, was Jim's wife Mary, a formidable fisher so I'd been led to believe. What I was about to see left me in no doubt. No sooner had I sat on the grass than Mrs Miller lost a fish and hooked another almost immediately. I was well wrapped up which was a blessing because the sun had gone behind the clouds. John Jacobs, the internationally renowned golf teacher, was wading from the far bank. Unless you're wearing thermals, wading can be miserably cold.

I was a bit envious watching Mrs Miller, I must admit. She continued to play the fish from the boat while the ghillie rowed her to

the bank. It looked like a twelve to fourteen pounder but was it a cockfish or a hen? They have a policy of putting hens back on this river. There's a bit of a debate about whether one cock salmon will cover more than one hen. Mrs Miller thinks it will, so she feels she's doing good by putting hens back. At any rate, her first fish of the morning was a cock salmon and an absolute corker.

She had four more while I was there. Neither John Jacobs nor Lord Aylesford under the bridge had very productive sessions. Only one fish between them. When I fished here with Ian Botham my wife, Pat, was also in the boat. She loved it but her touch deserted her. To be fair, she isn't an angler.

The great thing about fishing a pool like the Junction in autumn is that you know you're fishing on top of salmon. If you don't see fish your concentration can waver a bit. Some people claim they can *smell* fish in a river. I don't claim that but I do think that if you fish a lot you can learn to sense when there are salmon in the river. Smell is reckoned to be one of the salmon's strongest senses. That's how the pheromone theory you'll read about later first started. They probably do a lot of smelling at the Junction, trying to decide whether they belong up the Teviot or the Tweed.

Salmon have good eyesight too. Although they don't feed, salmon will go for things which shine or move, or both. Sometimes you can hook them with a piece of carrot or a lump of silver paper. The Tweed is a fly only river. The tubes they tend to use don't look like flies at all but as long as they don't spin that's okay.

A week in Mrs Miller's boat would cost you £5,000 for a single rod in early November. It's well worth it but on a pool like this I'd expect to catch a couple of fish a day. One of the guys in the hotel bar insisted the catching of salmon was almost immaterial. I think he's fooling himself. If you're paying that much money you can't help wanting a few fish on the bank. Of course, part of the fun is enjoying the scenery, the fresh air and the conviviality but the main

MARY MILLER WAS UNBEATABLE ON THE JUNCTION POOL...

part is pitting your wits against the fish. I like to try different methods, a sinking line or a small fly on a floater, for example.

When you're lucky enough to catch a fish it's the 'take' that counts more than the playing of the fish. If you've been fishing for hours, even days, with no joy and all of a sudden the line pulls, there's no feeling to compare with it. Then it's a case of setting your hook and praying. Mrs Miller could get into a forty pounder for all she knows. It could pull the boat and everything in it a mile down the river! With the greatest respect to her and every fisherman in her position, the assistance of a good ghillie is paramount. All the angler does, having selected his or her fly, is throw it into the water. Then the ghillie takes over. He keeps the boat steady, knows exactly where he is in relation to the bank and, most important, waits for the fish to be in the right position to net rather than chasing it. Never chase a fish.

One of Mrs Miller's catches went back because it was a hen and, obviously, full of eggs at this time of year. It gives you a great deal of satisfaction to put a fish back. Best not to hurry it. I once spent twenty minutes up to my knees in water trying to coax back to life a salmon that was played out, moving it backwards and forwards in the water until the strength returned. Then it was away to fight another day.

At the height of the industrial revolution the woollen mills which gave the Tweed its name helped to turn it into a polluted river. So things remained until recent years when the clean-up began, as it has in many British rivers. Now it's one of the cleanest in Britain. The water was running beautifully clear while I was there. Mrs Miller's ghillie, Gavin, said that the colour had dropped out and it had come into tip-top shape a couple of days earlier.

While the fishing party opened a bottle of Scotch and tucked into their duck sandwiches, Gavin got on with the weighing. Five fish had been taken in the morning, four of them by Mrs Miller. They were excellent specimens, between eight and twelve pounds. Not particularly big but noticeably silver. One or two had sea lice, which was a sure sign they'd only been in the river for a couple of days. The biggest fish of the day so far was twenty-four pounds, caught by Jim Miller, and it was unlikely to be bettered for weight. It had started to take on a rosy hue, indicating that it wasn't as fresh run as the others. There were marks on the upper body which could well have been caused by seals. They take a lot of salmon out of the nets of the drift fishermen of the estuary. Occasionally the sea fishermen catch seals in their nets. They don't like the seals because they eat or injure the salmon. People who love seals should understand that because they have no real predators they multiply endlessly if they're not controlled. There are enormous populations of them around the coasts of England and they do a lot of damage.

In the warmth of the fishing hut the whisky was going down a treat. Jim played down his wife's performance:

'You were very lucky. It doesn't happen every day. She was casting well. A sinking line with a big tube but there's a lot of luck involved too.'

Did he believe women had a magical power over salmon?

'I'm blowed if I know,' he laughed. 'The more you fish for salmon the less you know about it.'

What a marvellous position to be in. Actually *owning* the best salmon beat in Britain, possibly the world. I felt privileged just to be there watching. Jim's company leased it in 1971 from the Duke of Roxburghe at Floors Castle. That carried on for several years until the old duke died. The family had death duty problems so Guy, the new duke, invited Jim to buy the Junction outright.

'Reluctantly we did,' he says with tongue in cheek.

The best deal he ever did in his life?

'Could be – provided the salmon stay here. Otherwise we'll have the most expensive coarse fishery in Britain!'

I bade them goodbye until the evening so that I could continue my helicopter ride upstream. The sun had fought its way through again and the fields and woods were bathed in that lovely afternoon light you get in autumn.

A few miles further up the Tweed we came to the part I know best, Beamerside. The river runs into a very steep valley which I'd never seen from the air before. We flew over a beat called Sangsters. I've played and landed many fish there. It's possibly one of the worst areas to wade in the whole river. There's a part called 'the Dish' where the river bed is shaped as the name implies. I've fallen in there half a dozen times. One of the beauties of fishing this river is that you see salmon moving all the time, jumping at your feet or above and below you. When you catch at Beamerside the fish tend to be more coloured than at the Junction because the longer they've been in the river the redder and blacker they get. Fishermen

... EVEN HER HUSBAND JIM (*LEFT*) WAS AMAZED – AND HE OWNS THE BEAT, LUCKY CHAP

don't get a great return for their money but they still come at this time of year because it's a joy to fish in an unspoiled valley. This is where I first brought Pat to fish in order to discourage her. It was a very frosty day and I made her wade. She was back inside ten minutes complaining that it was too cold. Now when I ask her if she wants to go fishing she says 'no!'.

SIR WALTER WAS A BIT NAUGHTY WHEN HE WENT FISHING

We circled over Abbotsford House to have a closer look at the fabulous house Sir Walter Scott built for himself right on the river bank. With its walled gardens down to the water, it made me wish I'd been born a lord. I always wanted a place like this. I consoled myself by thinking that it might be the draughtiest hole in the world! I had an appointment with Sir Walter's great, great, great granddaughter, Patricia Maxwell-Scott. The helicopter came to rest on the front lawn. If there's a more

PATRICIA MAXWELL-SCOTT, SIR WALTER'S GREAT, GREAT, GREAT GRANDDAUGHTER, AND THE HOUSE WHERE HE DIED

attractive setting anywhere in Britain, I don't know where it could be. Before Sir Walter moved in for the last fifty years of his life, Abbotsford was a little farmhouse called Cartleyhole. It cost him 4,000 guineas when he bought it in 1811 and he gradually turned it into the stately home it is today. He was a remarkable character. After studying law at Edinburgh University he became a barrister but the practice crashed when he was fifty-seven so he threw himself into a frenzy of writing to pay off his debts.

While he was at Abbotsford he wrote his most famous books, *Waverley*, *Rob Roy* and *Ivanhoe*. Eventually, the strain became too much, as Patricia told me:

'He worked so hard at the end that he was simply exhausted. He had a number of strokes and a cerebral haemorrhage but at least he spent the last weeks of his life in the dining room enjoying the view over the river which he loved so much.'

It's well known that Sir Walter was fond of his country pursuits – riding, hare coursing, fishing – but not many people realize he was a bit of a renegade when it came to salmon.

He loved to poach using a very crude method I'd never heard of until Patricia told me. 'Burning the water' consisted of two men drifting along in a boat under cover of darkness. One of the poachers would hold a flaming torch over the river to dazzle and attract the fish and the second would stand poised with a five-pronged fork called a 'leister' ready to spear any salmon that rose to the light.

'He really enjoyed that,' said Patricia. 'When he couldn't use the spear any more he used to sit at the helm of the boat and hold the torch. Once he had to help a colleague out of the water by the seat of his pants after he'd overreached trying to spear a salmon.'

I turned up this extract from J.G. Lockhart's *The Life of Sir Walter Scott* in which Scott's great friend, James Skene of Rubislaw in Aberdeenshire, described their escapades. Skene, incidentally, was cornet in the Royal Edinburgh Light Dragoons while Sir Walter was Quartermaster.

GRUESOME TWOSOME. WHAT A WAY TO CATCH SALMON!

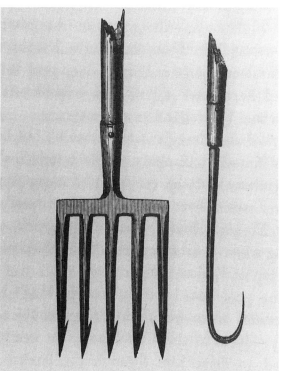

This amusement of "burning the water" as it is called, was not without hazard; for the large salmon generally lie in the pools, the depths of which it is not easy to estimate with precision by torchlight . . . I remember the first time I accompanied our friend (Sir Walter) he went right over the gunwale and had I not accidentally been at his side and made a successful grasp at the skirt of his jacket as he plunged overboard, he must at least have had an awkward dive for it.

All of this was illegal even then. When Gerry the boatman invited me on to the water to try my hand I could see that it must have been great fun. We borrowed a 'leister' from the display cabinet at Ednam House. Weighed a ton. No wonder Sir Walter grew weary of being the spearman and chose to hold the torch in his latter years. It must have been a cruel way to catch fish but a lot of people did it. These days poachers use much less demanding methods. Gerry told of a man he caught spinning at Abbotsford three years ago. The poacher was arrested at ten minutes to midnight having been released from prison for a similar offence less than an hour earlier! Apparently he came quietly. I had to admit that if I lived around Abbotsford, Gerry would have a hell of a job to keep me from poaching. I'd be sneaking down for a quick spin when no one was looking. Even if the bailiffs were there they'd have to catch me – and I can run faster than most!

Alongside the road bridge only 500 yards from Sir Walter's house was the scene of an awful tragedy on the Tweed in 1723. A ferryman taking a wedding party from Gallashiels across the river tried to cram too many on to the boat – thirty-three people and a horse. He tied his rope around a big tree but the river had been rising steadily all afternoon and the rope snapped. Eighteen people drowned. The spot is called 'Dead Water'. We sometimes forget that they didn't have so many bridges in the eighteenth century. Ferries were the only means of getting across. Several boatmen made a living out of it along the Tweed. This particular one probably

THE GHILLIE DOES MOST OF THE HARD WORK. ANOTHER ONE NETTED ON UPPER FLOORS

couldn't believe his luck when the wedding party turned up and that's why he tried to take so many at once.

Back at the Junction Jim Slater was into a fish downstream of Kelso bridge. He was making use of the last few minutes of available light, a combination of setting sun and silvery moon. Often dusk is a good time to catch. Jim is a very stylish fisherman. He casts a lovely line and he was playing the fish superbly. A nonchalant approach, letting the salmon go when it wanted to go, bringing it in when it relaxed. No pressure at all. The end product was disappointing. Jim's fish was more coloured than he'd hoped so back it went. He was fishing with a tube fly and had lost two during the morning while wading. His afternoon in the boat had worked out much better. For one thing he hadn't been so cold; for another he caught four salmon. Fishermen never know when to call it a day though.

'Must get one more before I go,' said Jim in the gathering gloom. 'Got a taxi coming in ten minutes.'

A light mist was forming over the water. I figured it was time to get back to the hotel where sportsmen would be arriving with their catches from all parts of the river. That's always a great time. The log fire crackles in the hearth, there's the smell of waxed jackets and wet waders and you sip whisky and wisecrack. The first person to check in was a well-educated lady from Berkshire and her husband, Roger, who emptied three healthy salmon on to the stone floor of the hotel foyer.

'A pretty good day,' she said in a slightly clipped voice, 'but not as good as two weeks ago.'

'Why, what happened?' I had to ask.

'Caught a thirty pounder on the same beat, Lower Floors.'

'That's nearly as heavy as you,' I joked. 'Did you land it yourself or were you assisted?'

'Roger helped too. He held the rod in case my arm gave out. It took one and half hours.'

Fishermen report to the main desk at Ednam House where they keep a record of every catch. I overheard the next chap:

'Three salmon lost but six caught plus one sea trout. The biggest is fourteen pounds. Can't grumble at that. One of the rods wrapped his line around a rock and broke it. Never mind. There's always tomorrow.'

Ever the optimists, anglers.

Most of the fish littering the foyer were cock salmon, in keeping with the Tweed tradition of returning hens to spawn. The underlying assumption is that one cock will service more than one hen, so cocks are dispensable. Is that right? It takes two to tango, generally. In other words a cock and a hen pair off; one lays, the other milts the eggs. When Jim Miller's guests started fishing the Junction twenty years ago, only the coloured hens were put back. However, they had such marvellous runs they took it a stage further, partly because a hen that's ripe with eggs isn't edible. Some people say that a cock *trout* can service a hen salmon. I guess we'll never know for certain everything that goes on in nature's spawning grounds.

The next question is what to do with all the salmon? They'll freeze them for you at the hotel and pack them in ice for the journey home if you wish. Pat always tells me not to bring any more salmon back. She gets fed up with them clogging the freezer. In any case, someone like Mrs Miller would need a hell of a big car boot to get her catch back! A good alternative is to have the fish smoked and sent on by post, although I think it's a crime to smoke fresh run silver fish which are much better grilled or poached. By the same token you shouldn't think that smoking is the best way to make a coloured fish taste better. A coloured fish is a coloured fish.

Smoking, as Fred J. Taylor will tell you, is nothing new. As far back as the ancient Britons they were using it as a way of preserving food for the winter months when hunting wasn't so good. I'd never had a close look at the process before so was pleased to visit a smart little smokery only three miles from the Junction, where they explained it to me. They got their business mainly from people from the south who left all their catches at the end of the week to be smoked, sliced, put in packs and dispatched. The smokery had only been built four years earlier, but the method was as old as the hills. Smouldering in the trays beneath the racks of salmon were piles of oak

RACKS OF SALMON AT THE TEVIOT SMOKERY. SMOKING GOES BACK TO ANCIENT TIMES BUT THERE ARE RIGHT WAYS AND WRONG WAYS

grey outcrop which looked like the profile of a woman lying on her back. It was christened 'Sleeping Lady' by Tinglit Indians who feared dreadful volcanic eruptions if anyone woke her up. So far no one has.

Standing there in the pale sun, which rarely pushes the temperature above sixty-five degrees Fahrenheit, I remembered looking out to sea from the terrace of our hotel on Italy's Costa Ligura during the World Cup. A much softer setting and a much hotter day. I remembered Tony Francis asking me in a television interview whether I envied the fishermen I'd been watching catch sardines in Rapallo Bay.

'No,' I told him, 'the Mediterranean's not my kind of water. I'd sooner be in Alaska.'

It must have sounded a bit daft but now we were here he understood what I meant.

You could almost *smell* salmon in the air, millions of them. Like the ancient Eskimo tribes we had been drawn here by the enormous runs of fish, but for different reasons. They were desperate for food to last them through the long frozen winters, while we were intrigued by the thought of rivers fat with salmon where rod and line men were guaranteed good sport. Compared to the Pacific salmon the numbers of Atlantic salmon are small and they have to fight their way through polluted river estuaries in highly populated areas. It couldn't be more different for Pacific salmon. Around Bristol Bay, which faces east towards the Aleutian Islands and the Soviet Union, *14 million* sockeye alone move upstream to spawn and die each June and July. What's more it's usually easy to catch them. Alaska has its weather problems of course but fighting the elements is all part of it. There's nothing like feeling the wind in your face, especially when the fishing's good.

There are five species of Pacific salmon. The smallest are the pinks which weigh between two and five pounds. Next come the highly prized sockeye which can be as big as eight pounds. They're silver in colour when they burst into the rivers but as they head upstream their bodies turn scarlet and their heads go green. They are the most distinctive of all the species and the most delicious too. Their delicate flavour makes them the most popular fish for an Alaskan barbecue and the most sought after by the canneries. Tins of sockeyes are the ones which fill our supermarket shelves.

Going up in size we come to the silver salmon which also carries the Indian name *Coho*. Silvers weigh twelve to fourteen pounds and take a fly readily. They are tremendous fighting fish which follow the sockeye run in August. The chum or dog salmon is next on the size scale, scaling up to twenty pounds, and the most underrated sporting fish of the lot. Few people eat chum although for some reason the Japanese love them. In fact they make caviar from chum salmon and sell it at £10 a tin. I'd never heard of anyone eating salmon roe before.

That brings us to the giant king salmon. *Chinook* the Indians call them. These are the big attraction. Thousands of fishermen travel to Alaska every summer dreaming of catching a king or two. No wonder. It's nothing out of the ordinary to net a fifty-pound fish on the Kenai or Russian rivers. The biggest I ever caught was a fifty-six-pound bar of silver on the Kenai when I was last here in 1988. The world record belongs to Les Anderson from the little town of Soldotna beside the Kenai. He caught a king weighing ninety-seven pounds four ounces in 1985. That's very nearly seven stone! We were to meet up with him a little later in our stay. He had a remarkable story to tell. You may think that nothing could top ninety-seven pounds four ounces, but let me tell you that an even bigger salmon was netted by the Fisheries Department in the same river. It scaled something like 120 pounds. I can hardly believe it really. It must have been in the river a long long time.

I suppose purists might complain that it's too easy to catch kings. Certainly you've got far more chance than you have of catching an Atlantic salmon in British waters, even the best ones like the Tweed, Dee, Spey and Tay. Also the skill level is not so high. But don't let's belittle Les Anderson's achievement. Catching a monster that size is a job for a hero.

Our first destination was the Alagnak or 'Branch' river on the edge of Katmai National Park, a huge river system discovered by the Eskimos hundreds of years ago. The second run of kings was due there and the chum were also reported to be plentiful. The Alagnak is out towards Bristol Bay in the south-west of Alaska. There was no base camp, just a small Indian settlement where one well known family traditionally moved down for the summer. 'Summer', we were warned, did not mean the same here as it did in England.

Katmailand Air Incorporated would take us on the one and a half hour flight from Anchorage. The owner, Ray Petersen, eighty-two years old, looked a bit worried when we stepped into his office. He knew he had to airlift four people and a pile of camera equipment but he wasn't expecting heavy-weights.

'You're not from Texas by any chance?' he joked as he made us stand on the scales one by one. 'I thought it was only Texans who grew this big!'

The cameraman scaled nearly seventeen stone and our total weight of sixty stone, near as damn it, made Ray pause for thought.

'We could make it in two hops if necessary,' I suggested.

Luckily, the film gear wasn't as heavy as he thought and Ray assured us the twin-engined Navajo would manage.

Ray is one heck of a character. He's of Danish

FLOAT PLANES RULE IN ALASKA. WE HAD SOME HAIRY TRIPS I CAN TELL YOU. MOST PILOTS DON'T EVEN BOTHER WITH NAVIGATIONAL AIDS. TAKE A WRONG TURNING AND YOU COULD BE IN REAL TROUBLE

descent, which isn't so surprising. It was a Dane called Vitus Bering who discovered Alaska at Kayak Island in 1741, opening up a new world for his employer, the Czar of Russia. The English were one of several nations who explored this frozen outpost but Russia ruled it for over a century and used it to develop her trade routes with Hawaii, China and California. Then in 1867 the Americans bought Alaska from Russia. What a good deal it turned out to be. Now Alaska provides the USA with something like a third of its oil. Ray Petersen and his colleagues established their base at a place called Kulik well before the Katmai peninsula was declared a national park. No one else will be allowed to establish themselves there so Katmailand Inc. has a valuable monopoly on all the fishing trips in that area.

Sitting in the little office he runs with his son, Ray told me how he made his first solo flight over Katmai in April 1934, when the population of the entire state was only 60,000. Half were Caucasian, the rest were Aleuts, Eskimos, Athabascans, Chugach and Tinglit Indians. The only fishing in those days was in Bristol Bay watershed itself, already recognized as the world's largest spawning ground for sockeye. The lakes contained millions of salmon but nobody had given a thought to sport fishing because unless you were a gold prospector on the Yukon, you would not dream of going to Alaska.

As a result, the area developed some of the finest rainbows, grayling, arctic char, pike and salmon you could imagine. Getting there in those early days wasn't easy. It needed nerves of steel and a good local knowledge, as Ray explained:

'The planes we used in the 'thirties were already four to five years old – Travelairs, Fairchild 71s, Belankas, Curtis Robins, etc. – and you have to remember there was no radio communication. When you set out on a three hundred-mile trip across the mountains you had to second-guess the weather. Most of the mountains were uncharted. All you had on the

map were big blanks! You had to know the country to fly it.'

It doesn't bear thinking about. If you broke down there'd be no one to help you. No rescue service then, not that there's much now either. I wanted to know if Ray ever left his plane, but he went pale at the thought and barked his reply:

'I never walked out. A smart man never walked. He stayed with his plane until he was found. Get off the beaten path and you were asking for trouble.'

It was time for the talking to stop. I wanted to fish. The little Navajo did us proud and once we got above the clouds the views were spectacular from our cruising altitude of 15,000 feet. Jim, the pilot, was doing exactly as Ray had done fifty-odd years earlier, flying by memory and sight with no reference to maps or compasses. It was incredible.

We flew alongside a volcano which erupted five years ago. It was an awesome sight, covered in snow and half buried under the clouds. I almost felt I could put my hand out of the window and touch the snow. I thought of Ray's last words before we left:

'I flew these passes for years and I never knew what was five miles off the route. If I had engine failure and wanted people to find me, the only chance was to stay on course. Stray five to ten miles off line and you'd be a dead man.'

He'd obviously got to his ripe old age by sticking to his beliefs. Even so, he said, you had to have a little ginger in your life.

'Fear has had a lot to do with my longevity. There's nothing like being a bit afraid if you want to live long.'

The mountains and ridges gave way to flatter ground. There was still snow but what caught my eye were the forests of sitka spruce and the big areas of tundra covered in grass and marsh and little else. The forests weren't like real forests. They were made up of really skinny trees which looked young but were probably a hundred years old. The growing season is so short that it would take them that

HELLO CAMPERS! THESE WERE OUR HOMES FOR THREE DAYS AT KULIK LODGE. BEAR COUNTRY!

long to reach a height of ten feet. It was a strange sensation flying over land with no sign of man or any of his work – no houses, no roads, no pylons – nothing.

As we banked over Kulik lake I could see the little airstrip in the clearing ahead of us. A few yards away were the chalets of Ray Petersen's lodge. This is where we'd be based for the next three days. I thought Northumberland was wild and open, but I hadn't seen anything to match this! Bo Bennett, the manager, met us at the airstrip and drove us to the main lodge, advising us to keep an eye out of the window for bears. They were just starting to arrive for the season. We scanned the hills and woods but didn't see any bears. That pleasure awaited us.

We trudged into the main lodge, weary after a nine-hour flight from England across the North Pole, and this last leg of our journey. A big fire was blazing so we dived into the leather armchairs and took the chance to unwind. But better followed. They laid on a late lunch for us of black-eyed beans, chicken and rice with pancakes and hot coffee to follow. You'd have thought it was Christmas.

After a cigar, a drop of scotch and a little nap I took a walk along the lakeside to watch a couple of float planes returning to base. One group of Americans had been on the Alagnak where they'd had a wonderful day catching five kings. Conditions were good, they said. Our turn would come tomorrow. However, I couldn't help noticing as I stood on the shore that heavy black clouds were gathering in the west, and the waves started to pound rather than lap on the shore as the wind got up. When it began raining I decided to have an early night. Departure time next morning was 6.30 a.m.

We had to scurry from the chalets to the lodge for breakfast because the rain was coming down hard. The clouds sat low on the hills. It didn't look good. Even if we managed to take off, there was no guarantee we'd be able to land. We left Bo and the pilot debating the pros and cons while we tucked into ham and eggs served in the sort of proportions that only Americans seem to understand. I love a big breakfast. The chances were we would need it. Much to the disappointment of Pete, the cameraman, and Terry, the sound recordist, we got the all-clear to take off. We were warned it could be a bit bumpy. It was. Bouncing around in the clouds with almost zero visibility, I wondered what would happen if the pilot took a wrong turning. Surely he'd never find his way back again?

Suddenly there it was on the other side of a wooded ridge, the Alagnak river, about fifty yards wide and flowing fast. When we landed I could see why. Torrential overnight rain had caused it to overflow. Our two fishing guides (they don't call them ghillies in the USA) said they'd never seen the river so high. It could be a couple of hours before we caught a fish. The water level needed to settle. Off we headed a mile or so upriver in two flat-bottomed boats

which really zapped along. I counted five other fishing parties but we were like dots on the landscape. Sitting in the boat and trolling a line off the side gave me a chance to size up our surroundings. Flat country. A few silver birches and those stunted sitkas lined the river here and there, but otherwise it was featureless, apart from one bare sandstone cliff about fifteen feet high. There were no banks as such. Instead, the river was overgrown with reeds. You couldn't get out and stand on the shore if you wanted to.

There wasn't much action until about 9 a.m. By then the water had dropped and the boatmen, Wayne Hansen (another American Dane) and Jack Duncan, guided us to what they thought would be the prime spot. Within minutes I felt a bump, bump on the line. Had I actually broken my duck at last? I'd fished all over Britain and Norway this season and not even had a salmon on. One look at the strain on the line confirmed my hopes. This was certainly a king. It proved to be a very strong fish too. I did everything right. I allowed it

PLAYING A KING SALMON ON THE ALAGNAK. HERE WE REALLY WERE IN THE MIDDLE OF NOWHERE. LOOK AT THE BEND IN THAT ROD

YOU GET ALL TYPES OF SALMON UP THE ALAGNAK. THIS IS A
SOCKEYE BEING BEACHED. SEE THE STUNTED TREES IN THE
BACKGROUND?

some line when it felt frisky and went plunging around the back of the boat, and reeled it in and pulled the rod up when it went quiet. Then we saw it. A breathtaking splash of pink and silver. It looked as big as a shark! I guessed around thirty-eight to forty pounds. What a terrific feeling it is trying to dominate a creature that size. There was no point getting excited too soon however. It had a lot more fight in it, more than I bargained for.

Wayne eventually netted the salmon a good twenty-five minutes after it took the lure. I was knackered, but my goodness it was worth it. It was perhaps not quite as heavy as I

expected – more like thirty pounds – but a wonderful specimen. I told Wayne to put him back. You're only allowed one king a day on the Alagnak. I decided to wait till the end of the day and take a chance on catching a bigger fish. It wasn't long before I caught a couple of chum salmon as well. To be honest I couldn't see why Bo rated them so highly as fighting fish. These two came easily. I wasn't even fly fishing specifically for them. I still had the lure on.

By now it had turned cold. The rain was slanting at forty-five degrees and we were glad we'd had the foresight to bring our waxed jackets, scarves and hoods. Life on the Alagnak would have been unbearable without them. What must it be like in spring and autumn, never mind winter? My watch said 10.30 a.m. Here we were in the back of beyond with no shelter, no means of getting out of the boat, no public toilets. And the pilot wasn't collecting us until 5.30 p.m. When the fishing's good you can go for hours on the bitterest of days and not even notice the weather. The only thing to do was settle down for some more kings.

Something quite astonishing happened next. Tony, the series producer, who had never fished in his life, decided the best way to beat the weather was to abandon his television duties for a while and dangle a line over the side of the boat more in hope than anything else. He must be the jammiest angler alive. It only took him twenty minutes to catch his first fish – a thirty-seven-pound king. He asked me to talk him through it because he didn't have a clue what to do once it was on the end of the line. It wasn't easy shouting instructions into the wind from another boat thirty yards away but he managed well enough. You're not likely to lose such a big fish once he's on – not unless your arm gives out.

We had a good laugh watching his expression when the fish first broke the surface. It was a giant. Jack the guide netted it skilfully and held it aloft for us all to admire. Wonderful fish. That one he had to keep.

We seemed to have struck a rich seam. Tony caught another king and two chum, and Terry, the sound man, caught and kept a superb silver king of about thirty pounds. I had a field day, three more chum and two more kings. We kept ourselves going with the chicken and cheese sandwiches they'd packed for us at the lodge, and cans of Budweiser that didn't exactly keep out the cold and threatened to send us looking for toilets which didn't exist! The skies looked more menacing than ever as Jack directed his boat towards a little bit of cover under a leaning birch tree and proceeded to fillet Tony's thirty-seven pounder. All part of a fishing guide's job. Most visitors want to take their catch home afterwards so it's put into the deep freeze back at the lodge.

Jack did an expert job in the blink of an eye, washing the fillets in the river water as he went. There aren't many rivers in Britain where you'd want to do that.

King salmon provide tasty flesh though not quite as good as sockeye, or 'reds' as the locals refer to them. Funny thing though, the price of salmon was actually going down in Alaska while we were there. Hundreds of commercial fishermen in Bristol Bay were on strike that very week because the canneries weren't paying them what they wanted. Two years ago they were being offered $2 per pound weight. Last year that dropped to $1 and now it had slumped to 47 cents. The reason was that the Japanese had a grip on the market. They owned three-quarters of all the Alaskan canneries as well as the processing boats so they could set the prices. Wayne, a native Californian who'd been taking sport fishermen out on the Alagnak for four years, was upset and concerned about the future:

'The Japanese drift nets on the high seas are taking all our fish. It's illegal but they still do it. They go into areas they're not supposed to enter with thousands of trawlers and they spread each net over a thirty-mile zone. They sail in there between Alaska and Russia where all the steelheads and salmon are raised. They do it deliberately, taking fish from the feeding grounds which is the one place that should be left alone. They'll tell you they're squid netting, but we all know that's a smokescreen. The boats are monitored by our satellite but they turn off their radar and disappear for two or three days at a time.

'The UN resolution to ban all drift nets in the Pacific won't affect countries like Korea or Taiwan either. They're not members of the UN councils. If we don't stop them there'll be no salmon left for us. Once they clear the place and eliminate the gene pool, that's the end.'

The only people permitted to take more than one king a day from the river are the Indians who subsistence-fish, as it's called. Cold and wet, and more than satisfied with our day's sport, we gunned the boats down-

JOHN AND MARY'S SUMMER CAMP. IT DIDN'T FEEL MUCH LIKE SUMMER TO ME. THE SALMON CATCH LASTS THEM ALL YEAR

stream towards the pick-up point for the float plane. I wanted to meet the Indian family who lived nearby: John Tallikpallik, his wife Mary, his deaf-mute brother, known simply as 'Deafy', and another John, the grandson who helped them out during the season. Their camp had been flooded by a combination of rain and melting permafrost. It was a job to walk around without sinking up to your knees. I couldn't believe anybody would choose to live in these conditions. The settlement consisted of half a dozen tin shacks, a tiny church which was never used and a smokehouse where the couple, well into their seventies now, preserved all the salmon fillets for their own consumption. The buildings were linked by rough boardwalks, the one at the water's edge being especially precarious. One false step and you'd be in!

Next to the main living quarters (topped with a set of moose-horns) were the racks where the Tallikpalliks hung up the fish carcasses to dry in the wind. Quite a sight if you've never experienced it before, and I hadn't. John told me he was an Aleut, not an Eskimo. It was hard to understand everything he was saying. Nice old boy. A bit shy but he didn't meet many people, just a few pilots and the odd fisherman. I don't suppose many of them bothered to talk to him. He told me he had seven sled dogs and had to catch enough salmon to keep them fed throughout the year. All the food had to be collected in four months between June and September when the family was in residence. Then they would head for the outskirts of the nearest town with enough king salmon to see them through the winter.

'Isn't it cold and lonely in the winter?' I asked him.

He laughed and said it was his way of life.

'But here we are in the middle of summer and I'm soaking wet and freezing cold!'

John replied, 'You got light blood that's why. You too soft.'

He was quite right.

While I watched his dear old lady breaking firewood to stoke the smokery I began to think that maybe I wasn't as much of an outdoor adventurer as I thought. Or perhaps I was getting old. One thing was for sure, John and Mary were welcome to this existence. The sooner our plane arrived to take us back to somewhere warm and dry, the happier I'd feel.

We had another half hour to wait. The wind was howling; and the rain was smacking us in the face. Undaunted, young John the grand-son and Deafy leapt into their motorboat and zoomed off across the inlet to inspect the salmon nets. Deafy let out a loud giggle which he repeated every few minutes. It dawned on me that he didn't realize what a loud noise he was making because he couldn't hear it. He held up a king which looked in the region of thirty pounds and the pair of them brought it back to the camp. Deafy was still giggling as he took out an unusual carving knife, which fitted over his knuckles, and began filleting the fish with a real flourish. The roe he placed on a separate rack with the others – also destined for the dogs I assume – and he washed the fillets in the river. It was all over in a flash and as a bonus young John offered me the salmon's heart, which was still beating, in the palm of his hand. I declined the offer. What must it be like to eat salmon for every meal, every day of the year? A chap could get fed up with it.

Foul weather didn't disturb most of the pilots who flew us. This one was different. He moaned constantly about the low clouds which obscured his view on all sides, while paying no attention to the fact that we had been in driving rain for most of the day and wanted to get back to Kulik Lodge as soon as

possible. 'If it doesn't get any better than this, I'll have to take 'em back to the river and they'll have to wait,' we heard him say over his radio. We were getting a terrific buffeting in the storm but it had to be better than shivering at John Tallikpallik's summer camp. Eventually the lodge came into view. We had never been happier to touch base. As we landed a big brown bear was swimming on the other side of the lake. We could just make out the top of his head.

The next day we had a lie-in and a late lunch and swapped a few tales with some of the American guests. I also had a go at fly-tying at a desk in the corner of the lounge area before deciding on a little trout fishing in Kulik river just around the bay. The wild rainbows were extraordinary. I fished from the bank and caught half a dozen nice ones. Terry and Pete were boat fishing and I could see them catching a few as well. In October it's not uncommon to take fifty to sixty rainbows a day, weighing up to four pounds. It's a bit colder then but Bo told me they still get a lot of customers:

'The wind almost blows your head off but people like to get the true feel of Alaska.'

The memory of our evening excursion to Brooks Lodge will live with me forever. The Lodge has been built around Brooks river, about fifty miles from where we were staying. You fish there at your peril. No sooner had we got out of the float plane than a mother bear and her three cubs came bounding down the beach towards us at a distance of only 300 yards. We stopped to take photographs until the warden Perry, advised us to back off because the bears would stride right on through whether we were there or not. How right he was. We hid behind the bushes and they went past not twenty yards from our noses. It was a bit scary I don't mind admitting. Perry was to escort us to the Brooks River Falls where bears often congregate when the sock-eye are running. It meant a mile-long walk through the woods but before we got there the path took us by a deep lagoon with overhanging trees where an enormous bear's head stuck out of the water. We weren't sure what to do. Pete the cameraman didn't want to linger but Tony asked him to film the animal before we moved on. He's a hard taskmaster! For some reason this particular bear was eating reeds it pulled up from the water. Perry was mystified. He'd never seen a vegetarian bear before.

On we went, past a sign which read: 'Groups of less than four people are not permitted because of bear danger', and into the woods. The path was narrow and twisting with trees and bushes on both sides. Anything could be lurking. We heard a small branch crack sixty yards away and saw a bear disappear deeper into the woods. Was it safe to allow fishermen to penetrate bear territory unarmed? None of us was sure this was such a good idea after all.

'Guns are strictly taboo,' said Perry. 'Bears have right of way here.'

But what could he do to protect me if one came after me?

'Not very much. People come here at their own risk.'

Not a very reassuring answer.

Perry told us to make some noise, so there I was, the manager of the Irish football team, walking through the woods clapping my hands and calling, 'Bear, bear go away!' I shudder to think what my players would have thought.

'Whatever you do, don't run if a bear comes towards you,' said Perry. 'It could be a false charge. I've had a couple of those. The best thing to do is hold your ground. If the charge materializes, roll yourself into a ball and pray he goes away.'

There had only been one nasty incident at Brooks, when a fisherman fell asleep on the bank after wiping his hands on the back of his trousers. A bear came sniffing, smelled the fishy trousers, picked him up by his seat and took him into the woods. The poor fellow woke up and made the bear drop him by shouting at it.

IT'S NOT ALL SALMON. KULIK RIVER IS TEEMING WITH MAGNIFICENT RAINBOW TROUT. TERRY THE SOUND RECORDIST HAD A FIELD DAY

THE BEAR NECESSITIES OF LIFE! FABULOUS SIGHT AT BROOKS
FALLS. ALASKAN BROWN BEARS QUEUING UP FOR SOCKEYE
SALMON. THEY HAD US SPELLBOUND – AND A BIT WORRIED

We got more nervous as we approached the falls. We could hear the water thundering not too far ahead and saw a bear cross our path apparently oblivious to us. Was it safe to go on?

'Yeah,' said Perry. 'The platform's just up here. Let's get in quickly, shut the gate and get up the steps and then none of them should bother us.'

The view from the platform took my breath away. Above and below the falls were eleven bears all gorging themselves on salmon – or at least trying to. The novices stood at the top of the falls waiting for suicidal fish to leap straight into their mouths. The one that impressed me though was the big old boy covered in scars who lay half-submerged in the foam at the bottom of the falls, picking them off at will. No fishermen were allowed within

a hundred yards of the falls. That was generous. You wouldn't have got me within half a mile of what was going on there. The interaction of the bears was fascinating to study. Each had his or her own position at the waterfall.

According to Perry they were taught by their mothers where to stand and how to fish. They stuck to their pattern of behaviour, although you could see their tempers were stretched tight. They had little tolerance for each other.

I couldn't help feeling sorry for one of the bears at the top. He stared down at the rushing water as fish after fish leapt past his nose. Sometimes he'd make a half-hearted attempt to catch one in his mouth or to waft at it with his paw. The awful truth though was that he didn't really have a battle plan. We were mesmerized and watched for a couple of hours during which the old boy in the foam demolished three salmon in double-quick time, head, bones and all. The bear at the top must have been starving. At last fortune smiled on him. A sockeye dutifully jumped into his mouth. He probably couldn't believe his luck after all that waiting. He turned, holding the fish by its dorsal fin, and headed for the calmer water to tuck into his dinner. As soon as he dunked it in the water and tried to hold it with his paws, the salmon was off and away! Our unfortunate Bruno did that twice more before finally learning his lesson and holding his quarry in a vice-like grip.

Perry had never seen so many bears at the falls at one time. We were very lucky. Salmon was their main source of food and the high protein diet meant that they grew larger than the inland grizzly bears who lived on carrion and small animals. We suffered a minor shock when the biggest of the lot emerged quite suddenly under the platform only six feet below where we were standing. He grunted at us, a sure sign that he didn't welcome our presence. The wooden platform on which all our hopes rested seemed suddenly very frail. We had been lucky to witness a fantastic and unforgettable act of nature. All the same it was a relief to get back through the woods as darkness fell, and home to our beds.

As yet the bears were fifty miles away from Kulik, but once the sockeye and the silvers got this far upstream, they'd be on the scent. We'd already seen the advance guard. In the autumn and winter months the lodge is at the mercy of bears who can still pick up lingering aromas from the kitchen. Carl Ellenberg, one of the pilots, told us how he stayed over till November one year, completely on his own, to act as caretaker. Rather him than me:

'Several times at night I heard them sniffing outside my cabin. They just follow the food smells instinctively. It's nothing to a bear to smash a window and climb in. I learned to keep a gun and a torch with me because they're all over the camp at night. One night the sniffing was louder than usual, then the door started rattling. I got up, opened the door while making as much noise as I could. The bear was on the porch looking me straight in the eye. I screamed, he panicked and we both went our separate ways.'

Hunger will sometimes drive them to eat their own young. It sounds horrific, I know, but food must be desperately scarce in winter and they can't smoke and store the salmon like the Indians can.

Lying in bed that night I put thoughts of sniffing bears in the porch out of my mind but reflected on the futile life cycle of the sockeye we'd just seen being devoured at the falls. When the eggs are laid they have to stay in the river under the gravel until they hatch. The floods can come so easily in Alaska and wash the lot away. Assuming they get through that stage, the salmon parr fall prey to small fish in the river. The survivors stay in the river, hopefully for a year before going to the ocean. That's when the bigger predators dive in – seagulls, ducks, mink, weasels and big fish. If they manage three years there they come back to the river they were born in. The Japanese drift netters are waiting for them, and so are the Alaskan commercial fleets, the seals and the sealions. Should they escape that lot they have to put up with the sport fisher-men as well as eagles and martens. If *they* don't get them the bears do and if they should dodge the bears they make their way up the river to spawn and die. Seems such a waste. Their carcasses lie rotting in the lakes and river beds, a thoroughly undignified end for a handsome fish. There is some sense to that part of their story, though. The parr rely on decomposing adults for food early in their lives. It's interesting that all Pacific salmon make only one return to their rivers. Atlantic salmon come back twice, occasionally three times.

Still on the subject of sockeye salmon, we discovered on arriving at Soldotna to visit the Kenai river that there was grave concern about the numbers of fish heading up the Kenai towards the Russian river. State officials anticipated something like a quarter of a million 'reds' in the latest run and that spelled disaster for the river beds and lakes, which could become clogged with rotting fish. Alaskans were being invited in the newspapers to get on to the river bank with their dip nets and intercept 85,000 fish before they made it to the spawning beds. Imagine a situation like that in Britain. The question in most places is not so much what to do with all these salmon but where's the next one coming from?

Salmon, as you can guess, dominate everyone's life in the Soldotna area, at least in the summer. This is an altogether different environment from Katmai. For a start there's a road linking Anchorage to Soldotna, which becomes the capital's playground from June to August. The resident population explodes from 20,000 to 100,000 as fishermen converge on the world-famous Kenai river. It was a vivid aquamarine in colour as we came in to land. There's nothing pretentious about fishing here, which is what I meant when I said I preferred Alaska to the Mediterranean. If he buys a $15 licence at a tackle shop, any Tom, Dick or Harry can fish all day. For $50 you can fish all year. What's more you're *certain* to catch salmon. I wish it could be like that at home but it never will be. The best places to fish will always be the domain of the wealthy and privileged. The man in the street will have to continue taking his chance on less fashionable and less likely waters. If he can scrape together the air fare to Alaska, he'll be much better off there. Everything is much cheaper than in the UK, fishing, bed and breakfast, food and drink, car hire and petrol.

THE KENAI RIVER IS ALASKA'S SALMON PLAYGROUND

KINGS, SOCKEYE, SILVERS – YOU CATCH 'EM, FILLET 'EM, COOK
'EM AND EAT 'EM WITHOUT LEAVING THE RIVER

You don't have to go further than the river
bridge in downtown Soldotna to see the Kenai
in all its glory. Mums, dads, sons and daughters
stand shoulder to shoulder along the shore
casting for sockeye. They call it combat fishing.
Not that there's any competitiveness in it, just
that they're in permanent danger of hooking
each other and getting their lines hopelessly
tangled. It's all part of the fun, particularly if
you hook a big fish and it starts charging up
and down the river. You might take everyone's gear with you. Hundreds fish like this, all
in a line. They use a standard single hook and
a brightly coloured fly which they allow to
drift only ten or fifteen feet from the bank.
Because of the milkiness of the water the fish
can't see where they're going so they feel their
way up the edges of the river. As the lure
floats across the salmon it will possibly grab it,

which is exactly what was happening while we
watched. With another half a million sockeye
due to come up any day, it would be hard not
to catch fish. However, they don't hang
around very long. It only takes a week for
them to cover the seventy-five miles from the
mouth to the Russian river. Each fisherman's
allowed up to three sockeye a day under
normal circumstances. Maybe they would
increase the quota since there was a glut.

All along the Kenai there are fish processing
and packaging stations for people who want
their catches boxed and frozen to take home.
Fishermen think nothing of driving 5,000 miles
from Michigan or Texas. Some of them come
in those huge Winnebago campers. Fifty miles
an hour is generally the speed limit in the
States but you have to struggle to keep up
that speed in a Winnebago. Other drivers
curse them like hell. They're supposed to pull
in and allow traffic through if there are three
vehicles or more held up behind. That's the

regulation but not many of them stick to it. What a lovely idea for a holiday though, to take a leisurely drive across the States in a camper complete with microwave, freezer, television, etc., fish on the Kenai and drive back with a freezer full of salmon.

One chap we bumped into had been coming there for ten years. He was a retired Texan who said he'd have abandoned the prairies and come to live in Soldotna if he'd been a younger man. I think I know what he meant. After one morning observing the lovely family scenes and the quantity of fish being caught, I had serious thoughts about buying a plot of land along the river bank and having a house built myself. I'm sure it would be a good investment and something to hand on to the grandchildren.

These ideas were given a bit more impetus when we were invited to lunch at the magnificent new home of Bob Penny, the chairman of the Kenai River Sports Fishing Association. He has the most unusual house I've ever seen, made of pine trunks imported from neighbouring British Columbia. Instead of being sawn into sections, these were installed as complete tree trunks. The floor caught my eye too. It was made of chunks of slate about six inches thick with underfloor heating. Needless to say, Bob was a wealthy man – probably wealthier than me! He'd made his money out of the construction industry and, despite the sophisticated central heating he'd fitted into his mansion, he wasn't often to be found in Soldotna in the winter. Bob would be enjoying the Hawaiian sunshine by then.

The dish of the day was salmon. Not exactly a surprise that. These folk must have salmon coming out of their ears. Bob intended to barbecue a sockeye in what he called his 'own inimitable way', but as an aperitif he offered us gorgeous Californian white wine and smoked salmon on rye bread. I'm never too fussed about the bread so I had the salmon on its own. The next course was – wait for it – salmon. Done differently though. Bob prided himself on turning the unfancied belly part of

the fish into a gourmet speciality. He seasoned it with herbs and a touch of garlic. Very tasty. When Bob's wife presented us with the main course, salmon steak, we weren't sure how much more of this we could take. Perhaps they were doing it for our benefit, taking pity on poor Brits who had to make do with tinned sockeye heaped into sandwiches and garnished with cucumber.

Stephanie Green, the 'Queen of the Kenai', was with us. She runs the Alaska phone-in 'fish-line' and had been catching salmon on the Kenai since she was a little girl. Surely Alaskans get tired of eating salmon?

'Not at all,' she protested. 'You can make everything with fish that you can with beef. The kings we normally roast or barbecue with lemon and onions. Sockeye we grill or poach or smoke. We also make salmon sausages, quiche, meatloaf, soufflé, soup. We never get sick of it. I don't anyway.'

You'd be hard-pressed to find a better position than the one enjoyed by Bob's house. It was only fifty feet from the water's edge with terrific views in each direction. Every few minutes boats drifted by in midstream, outboard motors running gently to prevent the vessel being swept downstream by the very rapid current, three or four anglers trolling, lines at full stretch waiting for a king to take their spinner. A great place to live but what would happen if everyone wanted to build a house on the bank?

Bob obviously didn't want that and justified his own building by saying it was a prime position for him, as chairman of the Association, to keep an eye on the river. Then he detailed his plans to take special care of the habitat he'd been fortunate enough to inherit:

'People love the Kenai to death. They walk the banks in increasing numbers causing widespread erosion. That's what we have to control. Most of the baby salmon live within three or four feet of the bank underneath the overhanging trees. To protect them we're using only 100 feet of our river frontage for

Nothing could be further from my mind than football at a time like this. The Tweed on an autumn evening is out of this world

Still life. A healthy spring crop from the Tweed at Upper Floors, further upstream from the Junction Pool

Pacific salmon are a different kettle of . . . . Five species in all. These are the pinks which flood into Alaska's rivers around the end of July

What a sight! This is the sockeye, the best known of the Pacific salmon. The head turns green after a few weeks back in the river

I wish I could get the Irish forwards to leap like this! Another sockeye heads upstream to spawn. No matter how many times you see it, it's a thrilling spectacle

A lovely flow of water on the Tweed at Upper Hendersyde. The air's crisp, the sun's bright and spirits are high

fishing. We've built a boardwalk to prevent more erosion. The remaining 200 feet we are re-vegetating with bushes and trees so it becomes a juvenile salmon habitat. No humans will be permitted to walk there.'

The chairman wanted everyone else with a one hundred foot frontage to use twenty-five feet for their boats and turn the remaining seventy-five feet into a natural habitat. He warned:

'If we don't do that there won't be a fishery here in ten to fifteen years because there'll be no place for the baby sockeye. The mighty kings will disappear too. I want our children and grandchildren to go on enjoying the Kenai. What the government and the state can't do we must do ourselves.'

And so to the business of catching kings. Flushed with success after our safari on the Alagnak, we boarded one of the boats Bob had very kindly provided for us. By common consent, Eagle Creek was chosen as the most likely pool. As we raced off in that direction the rush of wind to the back of my neck carried a chill reminder that we were in Alaska and even a warm day is not as warm as you think. The conifers were much taller and healthier-looking here even though we were on the same latitude as Katmai, and in the afternoon sun it was smashing to see all the caravans and campers parked along the shore. There were long benches where you could gut and clean your fish and brick barbecues where you could uncork a bottle or two and enjoy a fabulous lunch fresh from the river.

We sped past huge birch trees with eagles' nests in the top until we reached a wide bend in the river where only a couple of boats were fishing a 400-yard stretch. This was Eagle Creek, where Dave, our boatman, said the best fish always seemed to be caught. Actually it's unfair to call Dave a boatman. He was a fifth-grade schoolteacher in Anchorage whose summer holidays coincided brilliantly with the salmon runs on the Kenai. Somehow he managed to manoeuvre the boat, give us tuition and fish at the same time.

Dave smeared the silver lures and the lines with a pungent salmon oil which he carried in a pot, then four of us adopted 'bouncing' tactics. That's a case of trolling off the side of the boat and bouncing the lure gently on the river bed. The only member of the team who did not follow this plan was Tony, the producer, who kept getting snagged on the weeds and 'losing the bottom' every time we drifted into a deeper part of the pool. Well, Tony was a beginner. To make it easier we allowed him simply to dangle his line. You never know at this game. A shower of rain came and went as quickly as you are reading this sentence. It left us with a magnificent rainbow. There is something different about the light near the Arctic Circle. It's bluer and cleaner. Fortified by cigars and Hershey chocolate bars, I sat back waiting for my first Kenai king. Could I possibly catch a whopper like Les Anderson's record fish of six years ago?

We'd been to meet him at the Soldotna Information Centre where the ninety-seven-pound four-ounce salmon is kept in a glass case for all to see. At first glance it doesn't look that heavy. On closer inspection you can understand how the girth as much as the length accounted for all that poundage. It was fifty per cent heavier than the British record, Georgina Ballantine's sixty-four-pound Atlantic salmon caught on the Tay. Les recounted the fisherman's tale to end them all:

'It was a cold May day with snow along the shores when I felt the fish take. I set the hook as fast as possible. It put up a heck of a fight. Took me three-quarters of an hour to land it. Then we did a pretty dumb thing. We drove it around on the back of a flatbed truck for six hours before we thought of getting it weighed. We just wanted to show it to a few folks. Eventually we weighed it because we thought of entering it for a fish derby. The feller who checked it said that if his scales were right we had a new world record. I didn't know what to do next. We weighed it on four different scales before it was confirmed. If the fish hadn't lost so much blood and got air-

TONY FRANCIS, WHO'D NEVER FISHED IN HIS LIFE, GETS HIS
SECOND BIG KING IN AS MANY DAYS – 38 LBS

dried on the truck, it would have weighed a hundred and two to a hundred and five pounds.'

My daydreaming was interrupted when Dave let out a cry of delight. He had a king on. After ten years of trying and failing on this river he had finally made it. While he wrestled with the fish, I took charge of the boat knowing that too much or too little acceleration at the wrong time could spoil everything. The cameraman was better at mechanical things so I was happy to let him take the steering wheel while I got ready with the net. Dave quickly guided the salmon to the side of the boat like the expert he is and I netted a lovely big silver fish which thrashed about like nobody's business. Dave let out a whoop of delight. Americans always do that, don't they? We reckoned it must be a forty pounder or more.

That whetted my appetite even more. Tony warned me that we were already twenty minutes late for our rendezvous with the driver who would be taking us back to Anchorage to catch the plane home.

'Give us a bit longer,' I said. 'An extra half hour could make all the difference.'

How right I was, although not in the way I expected. This time it was Tony jerking his rod back in astonishment. He didn't believe beginner's luck could strike twice. Nor did I. We'd been the one's 'fishing'. He was just filling time.

'Don't get excited,' he said, 'I might have snagged another weed.'

One look at the strain on the rod and it was pretty obvious this was a fish. A big one as well.

Dave was at his best, skilfully controlling the boat in fast-flowing water and telling Tony to make sure the fish didn't get its head above the surface because it looked strong enough to shake itself free given half a chance.

Tony and the salmon did several laps of the boat with the rest of us bobbing and weaving as we tried to keep out of his way. This was a tougher one to reel in than his thirty-seven-pound debut fish on the Alagnak. The mistake he'd made was jamming the end of the rod into his chest instead of his waist, making it much harder to control. He admitted his arms were aching. I told him to forget the pain. Most people would *give* their right arm to have a forty-pound king on the end of the line. From what I could see of it forty pounds seemed a reasonable estimate. The fish tired moments before the fisherman after putting up stout resistance for about twenty minutes. Now it really was time to leave the Kenai, even though I'd gone empty handed while a novice upstaged me.

Dave called in at a riverside gas station to fuel up and weigh the fish. His was forty pounds exactly. Tony's was thirty-eight. He was nonplussed and wanted to know what it proved. Could any fool catch a salmon when they were in the river? If so, how come Dave (who knew more about fishing than he could ever hope to know) had been unsuccessful on such a prolific river for a whole decade?

CHAPTER FIVE

GOD'S LITTLE ACRE

Until I took the soccer job in Ireland in 1985, I knew nothing about the Atlantic coast. Now it's my favourite fishing haunt and my second home. Naturally I'd heard of great brown trout lakes like Corrib and Mask, and I'd heard of Galway. Beyond that I knew as much about it as I did about outer Mongolia.

During one of my early trips to Dublin on soccer business I had a couple of spare days. That meant finding a good salmon pool and escaping the press and autograph hunters. Someone suggested I got in touch with the oracle on Irish rivers, a fellow by the name of Peter O'Reilly who worked for the Central Fisheries Board. Peter was only too happy to help. He thought long and hard before recommending the river Erriff in County Galway over on the west coast. He wasn't a bad judge. It was a three-hour drive across the Irish Midlands where 'motorways' are the equivalent of 'B' roads. Very charming, though it's no good being in a hurry.

When I reached the Erriff the views were worth the trip on their own. Majestic mountains flank the river virtually all the way along its twenty-mile course. It runs into the ocean through the spectacular Killary Harbour which is a fjord nine miles long and one mile across. Somewhere in the middle reaches is Aasleagh Falls where, the locals keep reminding you, Richard Harris fought his battle in the film *The Field*. A great plunge of water comes over the

granite rocks, some of it coloured orange and brown from the peat. After heavy rain – and there's more than enough of that – the fifteen-feet-high waterfall disappears completely. If you've ever wondered why this country's called the Emerald Isle, one visit to the Erriff will tell you. The fields and trees are the greenest I've ever seen. No matter how attractive the scenery though, the bottom line for all fishermen is *fish*.

Peter said he hadn't opted for the Erriff immediately. He cast his net all over Ireland but the Erriff came out on top because it had been improving every year since falling into decay in the early 1980s. The reasons for that are as unique as they are unpleasant to recall. It started on a sunny morning in August 1979 when an IRA bomb exploded aboard Lord Mountbatten's fishing boat in Mullaghmore harbour, County Sligo, a little further to the north. Lord Mountbatten was killed along with a young son of Lord Brabourne who at the time owned the river Erriff and Aasleagh Lodge. In fact the group had just finished their salmon and sea trout fishing on the Erriff and moved to Sligo when the explosion happened.

After that Lord Brabourne wanted nothing more to do with Ireland, which is very understandable. He put the river and the lodge up for sale. Both had remained in the hands of the Marquess of Sligo after the land wars in Ireland in the nineteenth century. The tenants got the title to the land, but the landlords kept the sporting rights as well as the fishing and hunting lodges. Lord Sligo later sold the Erriff and Aasleagh to Lord Brabourne. In other words, they passed to an outsider, a Londoner, which didn't go down well with the Irish. Absentee landlords became a target for vandals. What made it worse was that the Erriff had become one of the most poached waters in the country. Not surprisingly there were no takers until the Irish government bought the property for just under £250,000.

Here's Peter's view:

'It's an ill wind that blows no one any good. The tragic death of Lord Mountbatten indirectly led to the government developing the Erriff into a first-class fishery. I was sent here in 1982 and it wasn't a pretty sight. The whole river was run down and there were no fish being caught although I watched hundreds coming in on the tide after the floods in June, July and August.'

He knew it had potential though. Three things impressed him: the spawning beds which provided great nursery facilities at the head of the river system; the magnificent fishing areas further downstream; and the fact that the Erriff wasn't plagued by nets in the estuary. The government owns the water two miles out to sea so no drift nets are allowed. It means that fish which come within two miles can run straight into the river, which accounts for an awful lot of salmon. In 1979 the annual catch was seventy-one salmon on one rod and line, the ones declared, that is. In nine years that shot up to 885 fish, all caught on fly only. That is the rule on the river although other methods are permitted for an hour in the evenings when anglers have gone all day empty handed. Then you might see the odd worm being used.

Peter and his party got to grips with the problem of widespread poaching. They first set off from Leenane posing as sea anglers to try to assess the extent of it. They counted no fewer than forty-nine fixed salmon nets set to intercept the incoming runs of fish. He told me some of them were being openly serviced by the poachers who waved at them as they went by. This is how he described the rest of that expedition:

IT COULD ALMOST BE NORWAY. IN FACT THIS IS KILLARY HARBOUR, A NARROW NINE-MILE FJORD ON IRELAND'S WEST COAST

I LOVE THIS SPOT. AASLEAGH FALLS ON THE RIVER ERRIFF IS
ONE OF IRELAND'S LITTLE GEMS

'At the mouth of Killary Harbour our boat had to zig-zag its way through the maze of nets. On the high seas, two half-deckers were openly drift netting despite the fact that it was Saturday and nets are prohibited at weekends. The river was no different. Gangs of poachers swept the pools with nets as soon as a fresh run of salmon arrived off the tide. Setting up to six gill nets across a pool the poachers barraged the water with stones, stampeding the fish into nets. They then moved off to the next pool. Some of the river poachers moved out to the sea, observing that their fish were being intercepted by poachers in Killary Harbour. Rows broke out in bars between rival gangs about poaching on each other's territory.

'Along the river banks there were abundant signs of illegal activity – fresh scales on the gravel in the morning where a netful of salmon had been landed the previous night, stakes driven into the bank to which the nets were tied, nets hung out to dry. One indolent poacher even asked an angler to help him pull in a net which had got snagged on the river bed. Yet in that season of 1982, the only person prosecuted on the Erriff was a middle-aged angler who didn't have a rod licence. No one could remember when a poacher was last prosecuted. Some locals said ten years, some twelve.'

The Erriff may have proved easy to poach, but fortunately it also proved pretty easy to protect. The narrowness of the harbour and the nearness of the road which runs parallel to the river meant that the Western Regional Fisheries Board only had to maintain a reasonable level of vigilance to keep poachers at bay. Actually they doubled their protection of the water system and equipped the bailiffs with radios and night-sights. To start with, an incredible 551 nets were confiscated along the harbour and the coastline between 1984 and 1987. Several poachers were successfully prosecuted and some sent to prison. On the debit side, the fishery inspector, Sean Nixon, was twice seriously assaulted. He reckoned that poachers had been taking two-thirds of the fish on the Erriff. Now that's all changed and I look forward to fishing there any time I can. I've fished just about every pool on the river in the last six years and have enjoyed some marvellous days.

Just a stone's throw from the Erriff near Leenane, which is a tiny hamlet, sits one of the most beautiful little fisheries I've seen in my life. It's called Delphi, which is about as un-Irish as you can get (more on that in a moment). The Irish name is Bundoragha river

and it's only one and a half miles long. The fishery includes Finlough and Doolough which are salmon and sea trout loughs in the middle of rugged mountain scenery. I always feel it's the last really wild part of the Republic. Exactly my kind of country.

Still, it was a brave decision by Peter Mantle to leave inner London and set up home here. You have to have a very understanding and self-contained wife to live in a place which is completely isolated from the outside world. What you do when the children reach school age I'm not sure. Westport's the nearest town and that's nearly an hour away. Peter, who's half Irish, was on a fishing holiday when he stumbled across Delphi Lodge. It's a superb mansion at the foot of a hill and on the edge of a lake. The Earl of Sligo used to live there but when Peter saw it the place was falling

PETER MANTLE'S HAD HIS PROBLEMS AT DELPHI LODGE BUT HE'S INVESTED A LOT OF MONEY IN SALMON. I WISH HIM WELL

down. It proved to be the chance of a lifetime. When he told me what he paid for it I almost fell through the floor. £200,000! That was for the complete Delphi Fishery which despite its size is one of the best-known salmon fisheries in Ireland. The deal comprised the house, four lakes, the river, a thousand acres of land and several derelict buildings and cottages. In fact, it cost only slightly more than the two-bedroom flat they sold near the Arsenal football ground, which just goes to show how daft property prices are in the City.

The average salmon catch for the year was just over 100 but the numbers had been falling since a high of 153 in 1986. To make matters worse, sea trout stocks in the whole of the west coast of Ireland had collapsed even more dramatically. In 1986 on the Delphi, 1,281 sea trout were killed compared to 309 in 1989. Peter believed the fall was caused by the salmon farms and the infestation of sea lice. Like everyone else he was worried about the future but instead of waiting indefinitely for things to get better, he gambled £75,000 on his own salmon hatchery at the back of the lodge. I admire him for that. From what I could see he had the potential to produce millions of fish.

Peter told me he hoped to release 50,000 salmon smolts into the Delphi system in April 1991. Already 25,000 had been released with their tags on. He was hoping that within a year the fish would be about nine inches long and ready to be released into the sea. The following year, if everything went according to plan, they'd be about two feet long and entering the river again to spawn. That's when the fun would start, he hoped. I was sure he was on a winner. If only twenty per cent of those 25,000 salmon came back, he'd have 5,000 fish in the system which would be absolutely marvellous. That would turn the Delphi into an outstanding salmon fishery.

'I bet you'll be selling 'em up and down the coast as well,' I joked.

'No,' said Peter. 'Every salmon grown here is meant for restocking only. We refuse to sell

FAR FROM THE MADDING CROWD. TWO MEN AND A BOAT ON THE DELPHI FISHERY. LURKING SOMEWHERE BELOW MAY BE A SALMON OR A SEATROUT

them commercially. There are enough fish farms about. We're only interested in enhancing the fishery, not in exploiting the species.'

Having had a good look around I must say I don't understand why everyone in the business doesn't invest in a hatchery. Peter picks twenty-five different pairs of fish to make sure he has a good genetic mix. All right, you could say it's man playing God but I can't see anything but good in what he's doing. If it saves his fishery then it was worth every penny of his £75,000.

Delphi is used to problems of one sort or another. One of the most horrific tragedies in Ireland's history happened a couple of miles down the road. During the famine years nearly 400 starving people called at Delphi Lodge, believing they could get food vouchers from officials who were having lunch in the house. They were turned away and died in a dreadful storm. I saw the small stone monument which marks the spot overlooking Doolough. It was pretty creepy with the wind howling and low cloud on the hilltops. Hard to believe it was July but the west coast can be like that. Normally it's one of the best months to fish. Not this time.

Every cloud's supposed to have a silver lining but the word around Delphi was gold not silver. Yet another headache for Peter. At the head of the valley they'd discovered Europe's richest gold deposits and Peter, along with his 'neighbours', was campaigning to make sure the gold wasn't mined. Let him explain.

'Gold mining would destroy us and the entire local economy, which is based on the fact that we have clean water, clean land and clean air.'

I wondered why. Surely all it involved was panning in the water?

'That's *finding* not *mining*,' said Peter. 'Forget cosy thoughts of prospectors because gold mining on a large scale is a monstrous process. You have to tear up millions of tons of rock and crush it into fine powder, then pile it into heaps of dust before pouring cyanide over it to extract the gold. All of that is done on site so there's potential for massive pollution.'

Mixed fortunes then for the Mantle family but as we set off south to Galway, leaving this threatened valley behind, I felt sure that no one would be allowed to pour cyanide through the hills and destroy the fisheries and mussel farms. The second Marquess of Sligo would have done his nut. He was the one who gave Delphi its name. Apparently he was doing the grand tour of Europe with a few more boozy aristocrats when he was struck by the similarity between this valley and the home of the oracle in Greece. As Peter says:

'He must have been on the ouzo at the time because there's no similarity at all!'

The Weir Pool in Galway City has a tremendous salmon history. I love the way it's smack in the middle of town with the cathedral and the main bridge carrying traffic into the city centre streets right alongside. It's a lovely city, Galway. One of the most unusual towns in Ireland. It's a mecca for visitors from France, Germany and Italy. They stroll around the streets or sit on the pavements just as they did in the flower power days. No one visiting the Republic should miss it. I was tempted to buy a house there but in the end I thought it was getting too commercialized, so I went north to Ballina, but I'm only one and a half hours' drive from Galway so I can still get there to do some fishing.

They get tremendous runs of water on the Weir Pool. The river Corrib drains Loughs Corrib, Mask and Carra and sometimes in the winter all twelve weir gates can be open and water comes right over the cliff path. In the six years since I first discovered it I've had great days there, catching just enough fish to keep up the interest but not breaking any records.

There are difficulties though. The wading here's worse than any river I've ever fished. Fly fishers fish down one side among the big rocks and boulders. As you step in and out of the holes there's a big pressure of water on the back of your legs. If you fell in you could always save yourself by grabbing a pole on the salmon trap under the bridge but I've never fancied wading very much. I've seen a lot of people fall in. I've had a few near misses myself.

On the opposite side it's very hard to back cast off the path. You can't throw the line behind you because of the high bank so you have to throw it straight up in the air and cast out. At least it's the sort of fishery you can come and fish in your Sunday best. The path is normally eighteen feet above the level of the water, so there's no need to get wet and muddy. However, if you're lucky enough to hook a big fish, how do you get it out of the water? Simple. Play it downstream to the end of the ramp where there'll be someone with a net to scoop it out. That's the theory anyway. I never have any trouble getting assistance, but then they do treat me very well.

One day I was fishing down by the bridge and a guy on the bank kept shouting at me. I couldn't hear a word he was saying because of the sound of running water. He waded towards me waving his hands and yelling:

'You've got to come in!'

'What for? I'm at the best bit for a fly. Why spoil it now?'

'Because the whole town has stopped,' he replied.

I looked up and there were a hundred people on the bridge watching me fish. The guy said the centre of Galway was paralysed and the Garda were trying to get the traffic moving. I had no choice but to come out.

Funny really, the way the Irish react to you. I make a habit of picking up hitch-hikers when I'm there. There are always kids and teenagers wanting a lift. I'm choosey though. If they're clean and tidy, that's fine. If not, I don't want to know because sometimes a smelly one gets in and there's nothing worse. The youngsters

THE WEIR POOL IN GALWAY WHERE THE TOWN STOOD STILL
TO WATCH ME FISH

do a double-take and say:

'Are you Jack Charlton?'

'Yes.'

'Jesus Christ, I'm in the car with Jack Charlton!'

An old pal of mine on the Weir is Ned Cusak who used to work for the Fisheries Board. He's well into his seventies now but fit as a fiddle and as good a fisherman as he ever was. He started fishing in Galway in 1940. Ned's certainly caught a few salmon in his time but his most vivid memory is a twenty-one-pound fish he landed on the fly in 1986. On that river anything over twenty pounds is regarded as a specimen fish. It took him thirty-five minutes to land it in high water. He still says it was the highlight of his life. Ned took over as manager of the Weir Pool when the Irish government bought it in 1978. Most of the anglers then converted to fly fishing as the most sporting

way to catch a salmon. In the 1940s, when he started, fly fishing wasn't especially popular. Bait was the preferred method. Although he'd seen salmon stocks decline in the preceding ten years, Ned still waxed lyrical about Galway:

'This 200 metres of river is the most productive in the world and the water is clean enough to drink.'

The year 1991 was a quiet one, make no mistake. To be honest, I don't know of any salmon beat in Great Britain or Ireland where stocks *haven't* been down. To try to find out more about the problems, I had a word with Michael Kennedy, the manager of the Western Regional Fisheries Board. He was pretty nonplussed:

'Two years ago the fish were jumping all over the place. Something must be happening at sea which is parallel to the collapse of the sea trout. All along the western region, which is one of the prime regions in Ireland, we've had two miserable grilse years.'

I asked Michael if this meant that sea lice were affecting salmon as well as sea trout because I'd seen no evidence to support that.

'We can't be a hundred per cent certain,' he said, 'but it's a definite possibility. The explosion of sea lice is related to fish farming although that's hotly disputed by the farmers. Whatever they say, the problem with salmon and sea trout is most acute in the area from Cloone Bay to Galway Bay which is where we have the heaviest concentration of fish farms. Can't be a coincidence, can it?'

Up along the path by the Fisheries office, the morning's disappointment was interrupted when a fifteen-year-old lad, Fergal Cormican, suddenly got a bite. The excitement was almost too much for him. Not only was this his first salmon on one of the most famous pools in the world, but the moment was captured by television cameras and Jack Charl-ton was volunteering to net it for him! I grabbed the net and ran down the steps to the water's edge where there wasn't much room for manoeuvre. In the meantime, Fergal was about twenty feet above me trying to play the fish in fast-running water only thirty-five yards from the gates of the weir. He did well but it was touch and go at the end. While I reached out to net it the line broke. Another couple of seconds and we'd have lost the fish. When I carried it up the steps to him, the lad was delighted. A little grilse, about three to four pounds, but it didn't matter. It was just his first fish and no one else had taken anything all morning. For the record it was taken on a shrimp.

The only other successful angler that day had skinny legs and a long beak. Frank, the resident heron, was a favourite with the regulars because he was part of the furniture. Danny Goldwick, the angling officer, was one of his biggest fans.

'He's a very good fisherman. If he's not

SO THIS IS WHAT IT'S LIKE TO BE A GHILLIE! I HAD TO MOVE SMARTLY TO NET THIS ONE

FRANK THE HERON. PART OF THE FURNITURE ON THE WEIR POOL. THE FISHERMEN LOVE HIM

picking up salmon smolts he's got a roach or an eel. He's also a very friendly bird. He comes up very close to the anglers who love to see him feeding for several hours a day before going off for a rest.'

As Danny was speaking, Frank pounced on a lovely little roach and while we were admiring him swallowed the fish in three stages, first the head, then the body, and finally the tail disappearing down his throat. We watched the fish bulging in the heron's neck before giving up the ghost. Frank took a few swigs of water from the weir and started looking for the next meal.

Talking of meals, no trip to Galway would be complete without calling at what I consider to be the best seafood pub in Ireland, if not Britain. It's called Morans of the Weir, down an unpretentious cul-de-sac alongside an inlet that you would never come across unless you

were specifically looking for it. Whenever I can I always stay at a little bed and breakfast place nearby. Ireland has the best B&Bs in the world and it's nice to get away from hotels. The place I go to has three young sisters who perform Irish folk dancing around the breakfast table. Where else would you get entertainment like that?

What makes Morans so special is its simplicity. Whether you choose the oysters, mussels, crab, prawns or smoked salmon, all the food is fresh and local. Apart from the mussels in garlic butter, it's all served cold as well. Wash it down with a few pints of the dark stuff and you're in heaven! One or two celebrities have found their way there over the years. Roger Moore was making a film in Galway when he discovered it. The peace and tranquillity knocked him out, as did the hospitality. He was down at the pub nine days on the trot. More recently, Julia Roberts, the star of *Pretty Woman*, escaped to Galway when she got cold feet and decided not to go ahead with her

WILLIE MORAN'S LEGENDARY SEAFOOD BAR

marriage to Keifer Sutherland. While she was on the west coast, Morans was on her itinerary more than once. And then there's me. They can't keep me away.

About three miles down the inlet, the owner, Willie Moran, makes use of 700 acres of natural oyster beds. He reckons there's no oyster in the world that can beat them and he's not far wrong. While I was there Willie and I went oyster gathering right at the start of the season. The annual Galway Oyster Festival isn't till September so they were bound to be a bit tight. The estuary of the Clarinbridge river (which still holds a few salmon although nothing like the days when Willie was a boy in the 1950s), has just the right mixture of freshwater and saltwater. The shoreline is perfect too. A hundred and fifty years ago, during the time of the famine, the place would have been swarming with local people collecting shells off the oyster beds.

In December you can see the farmers in their small boats dredging for the oysters. Willie normally gets his supplies off them, supplemented by oysters from his own private bed alongside the state-owned part of the bay. That way they can have them fresh every day. I love oysters. Eaten raw with that sea salt flavour. Chatting away on the shore, I polished off half a dozen in no time. The young lasses of Galway had better beware! Willie told me about a customer of his who set out to find whether oysters really were powerful aphrodisiacs: 'The feller had fifteen dozen oysters in one sitting. I was afraid to ask him afterwards how he got on.'

I'm getting too old for them to work for me but I still love them.

You'd be surprised at how meticulous the Irish are when it comes to controlling the Clarinbridge oyster beds. The bailiffs go out in their boats around picking time making sure that the shellfish aren't brought in before they're ready. They carry three-inch diameter rings and the rule is that if the oyster shell passes through the ring it has to be put back in the water.

On top of that it's one of the cleanest bays you could find. Said Willie:

'We're so lucky that there are no big buildings, no industry and no pollution whatsoever. They don't allow housing estates anywhere near the water, because the oyster beds are more important.'

Dead right although they're fortunate they don't have a population overspill and a demand for new housing.

One of the joys of the west coast is that it's washed by the Atlantic Ocean not the dirty Irish Sea. If you stand in Clarinbridge or Galway Bay and look straight out to sea, the next stop is America.

I was eating oysters to my heart's content quite forgetting that they cost £8 a dozen in the shops. If they're so plentiful, how come they're so dear?

'We pay the fisherman £3 per dozen,' explained Willie, 'but when we put them into our own private beds there can be big losses because of excessive rainfall or attacks by oyster catchers. You can fire guns and scare them off but they're only gone for five minutes.'

We were surrounded by twenty or thirty of the birds having a whale of a time. The sun was just starting to get lower and the bay looked magnificent. Across the other side was Tyrone House, owned by English landlords in the early part of the century when Ireland was ruled by the English. Sad to say Tyrone House burned down. It stands there now empty and derelict which is such a pity because the position looking out to the ocean could hardly

OYSTERS, RAW, FRESH FROM GALWAY BAY. HEAVEN!

be bettered. The English owned all the oyster beds in those days too and the river was renowned for its salmon. Willie remembered how they used to net the river when he was a teenager. Once they caught sixty-nine salmon in one haul. No problems with the stocks then because there were strict regulations about fishing at high tide and during the night. Nowadays the big drift net trawlers out at sea have made a mockery of the Clarinbridge as a salmon river. It's also poached from mouth to source. Gone are those mid-summer days when you could look out of your window and see the fish leap. What I like about Willie though is the way he refuses to serve farmed salmon in his pub. All the smoked salmon is wild. Willie believes the taste is far superior. I agree with him.

Before we left Galway for Ballina I had to put Mr Moran through his paces. He was twice world champion at opening oysters. His record for thirty oysters was one minute thirty-one seconds in 1984 and he used a small pocket knife instead of a long-handled knife favoured by most of the competitors. The secret, he said,

was getting the blade under the muscle, then the oyster was free. We took a whole basketful back to the pub to test him. The shells were certainly tight, as we expected, but Willie made a good fist of it, opening seven in thirty-five seconds.

And so to the river Moy and the place I decided to make my second home, Ballina. We were staying at a bed and breakfast a couple of years ago and noticed they were building bungalows just out of town on a high bit of ground sloping down to the river. They were exactly the right size. I didn't want a big house because then you have the problem of finding someone to look after it. The bungalows were perfect and I had a strong affection for the town. Ballina's a nice little place with a beautiful estuary and I have a lot of good friends there. I joked with the builders that if Ireland got to the 1994 World Cup Finals the house would become a tourist attraction; if not, I might have to sell it!

The point about the Moy is the famous

STRAIGHT LINES! THE RIDGE POOL ON THE MOY IS MY SECOND HOME. I HAD A HOUSE BUILT AT BALLINA

GETTING RIGHT DOWN TO IT ON THE MOY. THE GRILSE COME
THICK AND FAST IF YOU'RE LUCKY

Ridge Pool right in the centre of Ballina. Another of the world's great salmon beats. On the top of the tide it's nothing to see six to ten fish moving up the river at the same time. A phenomenal sight. It's an easy pool to fish too. Mainly fly but when the water's heavy you're allowed to use other methods. The Ridge is, above all, a grilse pool where you're lucky to catch anything over seven pounds in weight. On a good summer's day there are hundreds of folk lining the bridge watching the anglers. It's amazing any work gets done in Ballina! In a 300-yard stretch of water, the Ridge Pool once produced over a hundred fish to four rods in one day.

It caused an uproar. Two guys killed forty-seven salmon between them but in my view they did nothing wrong. They simply hit on a good day when the fish were taking. The fact that a picture of them appeared in the angling press triggered off a right old storm and yet enormous numbers of fish are taken from the nets and fish traps on the Moy. What all the fuss was about I'm not sure. At any rate a bag limit of fourteen salmon per booking was imposed in 1990, and of those six fish per booking are allowed to be kept. That means three fish per angler. The rest of the day's catch is handed back to the government which owns the fishery. It sells them to contribute towards the upkeep of the river.

It's not expensive to fish on the Moy – about £55 for two rods for a day in the peak months of June, July, August and September – but it isn't easy to get on. They get hundreds and hundreds of applications each year and your only chance is that someone has passed on or broken a leg when your letter arrives. Fortunately I get on fairly regularly because a minister who shall remain nameless sorted it out for me. The result is that I've got two days on the Ridge Pool. I'm very proud of them and I'd travel from the ends of the earth just to be there. Come to think of it, I won't have to in future because I live there.

CHAPTER SIX

WOMEN'S TOUCH

Before we set off down the Kenai river there was a curious request from Bill, the boatman:

'"Ph" it for me, will you, Steph?'

Stephanie did as she was asked, rubbing her long, well-manicured fingers over the lure and the line before passing it back to Bill to lob into the water. I had to interrupt proceedings:

'Hold on a minute, what does "ph" stand for?'

She replied with a big grin on her face: 'Phoo!'

I'll explain. 'Ph' was short for pheromone which is a chemical released by one animal and picked up by another. It can make the second animal do peculiar things – like take the lure if it's a salmon. Pheromones are steroids probably produced by the sex glands and released through the skin. Women emit more of this smell (for want of a better word) and salmon appear to be attracted by it. That's quite likely to be the reason that women have such a phenomenal record of catching them. The three biggest salmon ever caught in the UK were all caught by women. They were all cock fish too. That can't be a coincidence, surely? Not when you consider the proportion of women who fish compared to men. It's tiny.

It was interesting to see Stephanie Green in action on Alaska's Kenai river. As you'll probably have noticed earlier in the book, the rules about females being the dominant sex when it comes to catching salmon *don't* apply to

Norway; at least there's no evidence of it. Nor as far as I know do they apply to Canada. Alaska was obviously different. None of our hosts knew anything about the records held by British women so Steph's conversation with Bill was entirely unprovoked. She told me more:

'I believe there's a big difference between the "ph" emitted by women and the "ph" emitted by men.'

'How do you impart it?' I wanted to know.

'I take the lure and rub it good. Sometimes I get a hook in my hand otherwise it's a sensual experience. Now I should catch a fish. On average it takes a man twenty-two hours to catch a king on the Kenai. It takes a woman ten hours.'

She was laughing and joking as she told me this, but she obviously believed everything she said. And as someone who had been born alongside the river and fished it twice a week at least since she was a little girl, I respected her views. Her record wasn't bad either. A lot of thirty to forty pound salmon, half a dozen around the sixty-five-pound mark and one of over seventy-six pounds. Did that apply to all women on the Kenai?

'When a woman goes fishing, there's usually some luck on the boat. Whenever the female sex is hands-on, more fish are caught. Also it's invariably the woman who catches the first fish if we go out in the boat with people who haven't fished the river a lot.'

NO WONDER MALE SALMON ARE ATTRACTED TO WOMEN!
STEPHANIE GREEN SAYS IT'S A SENSUAL EXPERIENCE. GEORGINA
BALLANTINE (*RIGHT*) KNEW NOTHING ABOUT PHEROMONES
WHEN SHE CAUGHT THE BRITISH RECORD SALMON

If I had any doubts, they were blown to pieces ten minutes later when we bumped into a seven-year-old whose father told me she'd caught a fifty-pound salmon that morning. I bet she didn't weigh much more than that herself!

The debate about women and fish started because of the exploits of Georgina Ballantine, Clementine Morison and Doreen Davey. Within the space of two years between 1922–24 these three women caught the biggest salmon ever landed in Britain and started us chaps wondering what they'd got that we hadn't.

I'd always wanted to visit Glendelvine Water on the river Tay where Georgina, a ferryman's daughter, landed the whopper to end all whoppers on the evening of 7 October 1922. I got my chance at almost exactly the same time of year sixty-nine years later. There was the 'Bargie' stone, just as she'd described it in her diary, a large boulder on the far bank of the river only a few hundred yards from the cottage where she lived with her parents at Caputh. The house has now become a Mecca for fishermen from all over the world yet, astonishingly, Sir Gavin Lisle, who owns the estate, has never got around to turning it into a museum. I would if it were mine.

She was a lovely woman, Georgina, and she only happened to be fishing that night because the laird was indisposed. I must admit I was just a bit sceptical that a slightly built thirty-two-year-old woman could fight a two-hour battle with a fish that turned out to weigh sixty-four pounds. Must have damned near broken her arm! I suspect the old man might have helped her out a bit. I know what it can be like with a twenty-five-pound salmon on the end of a line. The funny thing is, according to her parish minister, the Reverend Routledge-Bell, she could have gaffed the fish within five minutes. It came straight to the boat showing no fight but suddenly caught sight of the gaff and shot down the river. This is how Georgina takes up the story in her diary:

The fish kept running out a few paces, then returning . . . by this time my left arm ached so much with the weight of the rod that it felt paralysed, but I was determined that whatever happened nothing would induce me to give in . . . Once I struck the nail on the head by remarking that if I successfully gaffed this fish he, my father, must give me a new frock. 'Get the fish landed first and then we'll see about the frock,' was the reply.

Eventually her father, James, gaffed the brute in absolute darkness and Georgina went into the pages of history. Rev Routledge-Bell, 'Rut' as he's known, reckons the fame didn't change her. He said:

'She'd never mention the salmon unless you did first, and then she'd refer to "that dratted fish". She was shy in large gatherings and when invited to give a first-hand account of the catch at a dinner organized in her honour, she got her cousin to do it instead.'

There was a boyfriend around that time, but the British record holder was devoted to looking after her parents and turned down the offer of marriage. Her young man emigrated to New Zealand. Georgina had a sad few years at the end of her life. Both her legs were amputated because of the effects of arthritis. Wheelchair-bound she kept open house for anglers though and even collected discarded clothing for fishermen who fell in. This was in the days before waders and waxed jackets don't forget.

But let's look back for a moment at that record sixty-four pounder. Was it attracted by Georgina's pheromones? We must bear in mind that Georgina had already taken three salmon that day, weighing seventeen, twenty-one and twenty-five pounds, so it wasn't a one-off. I asked Rut if he ever discussed the reason for her prowess in a man's sport.

THE REV BELL POOH-POOH'S THE 'PH' THEORY

RECORD TAY SALMON, 64 LBS LENGTH 4'6", GIRTH 28½", CAUGHT ON GLENDELVINE WATER BY MISS BALLANTINE, 7TH OCTOBER 1922

I'LL NEVER KNOW WHY THEY DIDN'T TURN GEORGINA'S COTTAGE INTO A MUSEUM. THOUSANDS COULD SEE THE FISH THEN

'Yes, several times but I doubt Georgina would have gone along with this pheromone theory. She was a great believer in coincidence. In any case there were more big fish about between the wars. It's been a steady decline since the 'fifties and 'sixties. I fished with her many times and she was good at it.'

That's as may be, but the evidence is there for all to see and I think it's more than coincidence. There has to be some other explanation.

Second in line to Georgina is Clementine Morison who caught a sixty-one-pound salmon on a fly in the Lower Shaw pool on the Deveron exactly two years later. Another point of similarity here. Just like Miss Ballantine, Clementine had killed two more decent-sized fish that day, each weighing sixteen pounds.

DOREEN'S CATCH INVITED A PROPOSAL OF MARRIAGE

Third place goes to Doreen Davey who hooked a salmon weighing fifty-nine and a half pounds on the river Wye in March 1923. Great river the Wye. When I was there in the month of June it was looking its best, although you'd have a heck of a job catching a salmon half that size these days. The runs seems to have dwindled to a trickle. Yet the Wye has had a reputation for big fish ever since a number of salmon were introduced from the Rhine in the mid 1800s to boost stocks. The German fish were big and their progeny among the biggest in the UK. When you look at the record of Robert Pashley you can see how plentiful they were too. The 'Wye Wizard' caught an astounding 10,237 salmon in his career. Twenty-nine of them were over forty pounds and in 1936, which must have been a fantastic year, he caught 678. The net weight was 10,888 pounds!

Funnily enough, the biggest fish ever taken

in the Wye wasn't a salmon at all, but a royal sturgeon! It was caught by James Postins in 1846 and guess what it scaled – 182 pounds! Let's be honest, Mr Postins didn't so much catch it as wrestle it on to the bank. He'd seen it in the river, wondered what it was and dived on it! It looked pretty much the worse for wear in the glass case at Hereford Museum but it must have produced loads of caviar. Why are they called *royal* sturgeons? Because a sturgeon caught in British waters has to be offered first to the Crown. I wonder what Queen Victoria made of it?

Doreen Davey wasn't born then so we can't put that one down to pheromones. Doreen's daughter, Mrs Ann Clay, was reluctant to tell us about her legendary mum but something must run in the family because she claims to have caught two salmon on the same fly at the same time. I've never heard of that before.

I fulfilled another ambition when I went to Cow Pond at Winforton to fish in the same spot where Doreen had her greatest triumph. It was a foul March evening with an awful north-east wind blowing when she came up trumps. The weather was beastly for me too. Trying to cast in a gale was hopeless. Doreen caught her salmon on a two-inch devon, spinning. I tried fly fishing but gave up.

Unlike Georgina and Clementine, Doreen had spent a cold and frustrating day at Winforton with no sign of fish until she turned to the minnow as a last resort before packing up for the day. On this occasion her father, Major Davey, definitely took a hand but that's not really the point. The main thing is who was holding the rod when the fish took. After a while the major handed the rod back to his daughter saying: 'It's your funeral!' Here's an extract from her account:

Then at last, about 7 p.m. he (the salmon) got quite cross, running down and across the river, wallowing along the surface so that we could see him for the first time. Up to now we had only been guessing but in the fading twilight we could see that it was really a monster reflected on the surface of the water.

The Davey's chauffeur, John Ellis, lit a fire on the bank to try to provide light, and the fish was finally landed one hour and fifty-five minutes after it was hooked. Doreen became a national celebrity, receiving poems from complete strangers and even a proposal of marriage. She didn't take that bait.

'This is another catch and I'm not rising,' was her answer.

As for the equipment she used, well the minnow was a two-inch aluminium made by Hattons in Hereford, the hook and mount from the same supplier. And the rest? Says Doreen:

The line was an old and ridiculously thin undressed silk supplied by Hattons to my uncle, Lieut. J.S. Davey, who was killed at Ypres in 1914. This line killed a thirty-four pounder in 1914 so you can tell it was a good bit of stuff.

I'M STANDING ON THE EXACT SPOT AT WINFORTON WHERE DOREEN CAUGHT HER 59-POUNDER. YOU NEVER KNOW!

What she doesn't tell us is whether she rubbed 'ph' over the line and the minnow. I doubt she did but she wouldn't necessarily have to if Stephanie Green's beliefs hold water. It's sufficient that a woman, preferably a young woman, ties the fly or whatever lure she's using on to the hook.

In order to delve a little deeper into the pheromone theory, I arranged to meet Professor Peter Behan, a neurologist from Glasgow Royal Infirmary, who's been studying it for several years. We met alongside the river Tay at Scone Palace where the professor, an inveterate salmon fisherman himself, drew up his boat for a bite of lunch. He had been wary of our conversation, unsure whether we were waiting to pour scorn on his thinking. I told him that quite the reverse was true. There's only one woman for every 200 male salmon

THE BIGGEST FISH EVER CAUGHT ON THE WYE WAS A
STURGEON — AND THAT WAS GIVEN TO A WOMAN. PROFESSOR
BEHAN (*RIGHT*) COULD WELL BE ON TO SOMETHING

anglers so by the law of averages they had no right to be top of the table. On top of that, smell has long been recognized as a vital way of communicating in the animal world. Lots of my pals won't smoke before they put a fly on because they don't want to take the chance of repelling a fish with the cigarette smell on their fingers.

Professor Behan says that research carried out here and in the States shows that women very often catch big salmon in clusters, three or four on the same day. (Georgina and Clementine both did.) On the Tweed the record is twenty-eight in a single day – by a woman of course – and the best example he knew was on the Conan where another woman caught thirty-six in a day, the heaviest being fifty-one pounds. He couldn't remember her name.

When we were on the Erriff on the west coast of Ireland, we found the gravestone of another great woman angler, Alice Marsh, who still holds the record on that glorious river

for a fish weighing 46 lbs. Consistent with the research findings, Alice also caught large numbers of salmon as well as big ones. In 1965 she took twenty fish in two successive August days, all on a fly and with an average weight of around 15 lbs.

Peter Behan continued:

'Women aren't better anglers. Men have greater strength. It's nothing to do with the lure so the reason they hold the records has to be sought elsewhere. We must stress that all the big salmon are males – they're almost bound to be at those weights – and the ones caught by Georgina and Doreen, not to mention scores of others around the world, were hooked during the spawning season when the male is at its friskiest. Information just coming to light in the USA shows that salmon have

receptors on the base of the dorsal fin and these respond to all sorts of different stimuli – saliva, ovarian fluid, even bile. Pheromones are strongly believed to be part of that group too.'

You may have heard about the experiments said to have taken place at an American fish pass where men putting their hands in the water drove the salmon back. When women were invited to dip their hands in, the fish carried on swimming through. If that's true, and Professor Behan swears it is, then we need to take this thing seriously. He was at pains to point out how a female moth for instance can give off pheromones which will attract males from eight miles away. It's certainly a fact that something about a woman can affect silkworms, so much so that in the old days they had to be very careful about having females in the silk mill. That's the nub of the thing in my

YOU CAN'T IGNORE THE FACTS. WOMEN CATCH A LOT OF BIG SALMON. OOPS – HERE'S ANOTHER ON THE SPEY

opinion. We know males and females of the same species attract but the idea of males and females from different species attracting each other is a new one. What we're saying is that cock salmon fancy women! Somehow I didn't think Arthur Oglesby would agree:

'Absolute hocus-pocus! We put women in the best spots and they have more patience than men, that's all. It's like sticking labels on jars. Grace, my wife, is a good fisherwoman but she doesn't have any unusual catches. If I asked her to fish a certain pool all day just in case, she'd be perfectly happy to do it. Women are like that. Men get bored.'

Georgina Ballantine's parish minister was even more dismissive. You could almost see the steam coming out of his ears:

'I think Professor Behan's theories are completely and utterly mad! I've heard of old gentlemen having strange ideas about women but it doesn't work when you're catching fish.'

'Come on Rut,' I said. 'There could be some truth in this. We all know that scent's special with animals!'

'So's coincidence. I can remember catching fifteen salmon on Stobhall beat on the Tay when my partner in the boat caught nothing. We were sitting side by side. What's that if it's not coincidence?'

'All right then, what about smokers washing their hands before they go fishing because everyone says it repels fish. I smoke and I've done it myself.'

'And did you catch any fish?'

'Well, I can't remember now.'

'Jack, you must be more gullible than you look. The professor would have to produce more concrete evidence to convince most of us.'

Arthur's argument that women do so well because they are in the best spots is a popular one. Remember from earlier in the book how well Mrs Mary Miller did on the Junction Pool on the Tweed. She caught five fish in the space of about an hour. No one else fishing the Junction had much success, but then she *was* in a boat in the prime position where the

ARTHUR OGLESBY'S WIFE, GRACE, IS A PRETTY HANDY ANGLER TOO. MIND YOU, SHE HAS A GOOD COACH! HERE SHE IS ON THE BALLYNAHINCH IN CONNEMARA

Tweed and the Teviot meet. How did Peter Behan answer that one?

'There are good examples of men spending hours on the Tay where I fish and catching nothing at all. When they pass the rod to a woman, she has caught a good-sized salmon in minutes. It's not about the best positions at

all. If salmon are in the water, it's the woman who will attract them.'

Off we went to the Freshwater Fisheries laboratory at Pitlochry to try to shed more light on the matter. Dr Richard Shelton is one of the UK's leading authorities on fish. He told me first about a young woman in Ireland who was looking for some thread to tie a fly when her fishing tutor, a middle-aged woman, said: 'Whatever you do, be sure to take it from your own tweed, not mine. I'm too old.' That story dates back the best part of a century, well before anyone had heard of Professor Behan or pheromones. So what was Dr Shelton saying, that the professor was right? He put on a video before answering. It was shot by the Fisheries Department and showed good underwater shots of salmon moving up to spawn. He stopped the tape to say:

'You see how it's always the males who

follow the females up the river and on to the redds. Once the cutting starts, the cock fish appears below, perhaps responding to the scent. Ovarian fluid is very attractive to males so there's direct evidence of a strong scent cue between the sexes. The fish's sense of smell is extraordinary. It responds to the nearest trace elements. What's more, smell travels well in water.'

'You'd think if that's the case that the scent would attract predators when they're spawning,' I said.

'Yes, but luckily the salmon doesn't have any big fish predators in freshwater.'

'Okay, doctor, what's your verdict on why women catch the biggest fish?'

'Well, to be fair to them, women have greater manipulative skills than men. That's why they're so good at things like knitting. How many men do you know who knit? Women are also more patient and gentler. With a large fish, that could be the difference between snatching at it and losing it, or taking your time like Georgina did and winning in the end. However, my feeling is that young women possess chemical clues which they emit unconsciously.'

Nobody had ever 'ph'd my line so I had to put it to the test. There was no one better to do it than Lynn Woodward, the only woman ghillie in Great Britain, whom we met earlier at Lydbrook Fishery, one of the most picturesque spots on the Wye. Lynn, in her early twenties, caught her first fish at the age of eight. Her father George, with whom she now works, bought her a small rod and left her beside a little brook in Shropshire where they lived. Suddenly there was a loud shout and George turned around to see a small child with a rod over her shoulder and a trout in her hand.

'She's a damned good ghillie,' he said proudly. 'She goes out at night with the poaching patrol. She's basically never known anything different.'

'I wouldn't mind being attacked by her at night!'

'You can go fishing with her tomorrow, how will that do?'

Very nicely thanks, George. As we got the gear ready for the boat, Lynn told me how she became a ghillie in the first place. A new chap bought the fishery and when the second ghillie left she saw her chance:

'I dropped hints to Dad, asking him if I could have a go because I loved fishing. He said he was having nothing to do with it. Told me to put in for the job. I did and I got it.'

'How old were you?'

'Nineteen.'

'I'd have thought you'd be more interested in boyfriends.'

'I already had one!'

'Seems a strange job for a girl. Do you like it?'

'I love it, except in cold weather. That really gets to me. The hardest thing was learning to row. Now I can do everything except use the chainsaw to clear up the banks.'

'Is it a job for life?'

'Yes, but I'd like to try another river soon.'

We were easing gently upstream with the smart little fishing hut to our left and a beautiful sloping bank of trees to our right. An idyllic setting with the sun breaking through the clouds. As always in June, the birdsong was deafening. Twenty miles or so behind us was Ross-on-Wye, ahead of us around a big loop in the river lurked Symonds Yat where the only way to get from the east to the west side of the village is by ferry. Lynn knew all the hot spots on the Wye, such as they were. From January to April you can use minnows, tobies, any form of spinning apart from natural bait. After that it's worms or prawns until the end of August then back to spinning or fly for the last three weeks until 17 October. I came straight to the point.

'Lynn, I just want *you* to handle my prawn. I don't want to touch it. I used to think women were good salmon anglers because of their patience but now I reckon it's all to do with hormones.'

She did as she was asked so I had no excuses

LYNN WOODWARD, THE ONLY WOMAN GHILLIE IN BRITAIN, GIVES SOME PHEROMONE ASSISTANCE AT LYDBROOK ON THE WYE. DIDN'T DO ME MUCH GOOD

now. Lynn didn't go along with the hormone idea.

'I fish seven days a week, but I don't catch any more fish than anyone else. I'm sure if you or any good fisherperson was here seven days a week, you'd catch as many as we do. If anything my father catches more than I do.'

'What's your biggest salmon?'

'Oh, nothing extraordinary. Twenty pounds.'

'That's not bad, you know.'

'For these days yes, I s'pose so. I lost a good one once which would have been much heavier, but I don't want to talk about that.'

'I find you forget the fish you catch. It's the ones you lose you remember most.'

'Dead right.'

It was perfect! I couldn't imagine anything nicer than sitting in a boat with a lovely young lady, fishing. So far it wasn't bringing me any luck but somehow it didn't seem to matter. I was surprised we were allowed to fish on a shrimp or worm. I thought the Wye would have gone to fly years ago. Lynn said the Flyfishers Association were trying to get a ban on shrimps. They might allow anglers to continue with worms. I thought of what Professor Behan had said, that the teeth on the roof of the fish's mouth puncture the worm and it's the scent of the worm that makes salmon swallow it. It doesn't swallow flies, he said. I think worms are one of the most exciting forms of fishing. Those who pontificate about fly only have never fished a shrimp or a worm. Lynn disagreed:

'I love fly fishing. It's nice to present a fly because there's more enjoyment in casting.

People get pleasure out of other people watching them cast a fly.'

'That's the point. I've seen guys with floating lines who'll never catch a fish in a million years but they like it because it *looks* good. I've even hit myself on the back of the head casting!'

'I must say I can't see the point of shrimp flies. If you can make a fly look like a shrimp you might as well have a proper shrimp on.'

I reeled in ready to re-cast but clean forgot what I was doing because we were so busy talking.

'Lynn, I've just touched my own prawn so all your scent will have gone.'

She laughed: 'Don't worry, Jack. To listen to you anybody would think I was Madonna! I think if there's a fish there and it's in the mood it'll go for it no matter who puts the bait on.'

'Yes, but what puts it *in* the mood? There must be some magic about women.'

'Possibly. The biggest salmon caught by a woman while I've been here (apart from me) is sixteen pounds but it's not very often that women fish.'

'Is that because the husbands know it'll cost twice as much to take the wife as well?'

'We invite people to bring a guest every three weeks but you never see anyone bring his wife.'

'I think it's a good sport for women.'

'Yeah, more women should do it. It's the same with shooting. Everybody thinks of them as men's sports. Lots of women don't like putting worms on but if you want to catch a fish you get used to it.'

'Couldn't agree more. When people say to me, "Oh I couldn't do that," I say, "Rubbish." You can learn to do anything. If your life depended on it you'd do it.'

The afternoon was wearing on. We thought we saw one salmon move but that was it. Not exactly a case of QED. To be truthful I don't know how you *would* prove or disprove the

WAS IT PHEROMONES WHICH ATTRACTED CHARLES TO DI? SHE NEVER REALLY TOOK TO FISHING OR BALMORAL. COULDN'T WAIT TO GET BACK TO LONDON

theory. Stephanie said that on average it took a woman ten hours to catch a king salmon in Alaska. We hadn't got ten hours to kill but as it turned out she caught two sockeye within half an hour of 'ph-ing' her line and talking to us. Admittedly sockeye weren't in short supply but the heavy run hadn't quite started and, more important, no one else around us was catching anything. You can draw your own conclusions, but let's give the final word to Professor Behan and the Rev Routledge-Bell. The professor first:

'Once the molecular structure of pheromones is worked out, the whole nature of fishing will change. Can you imagine how much easier it'll be to catch salmon with a touch of 'ph' on the line?'

'If Mr Behan put half a dozen dancing girls in the river and the fish started to take, I might believe him.'

INDEX